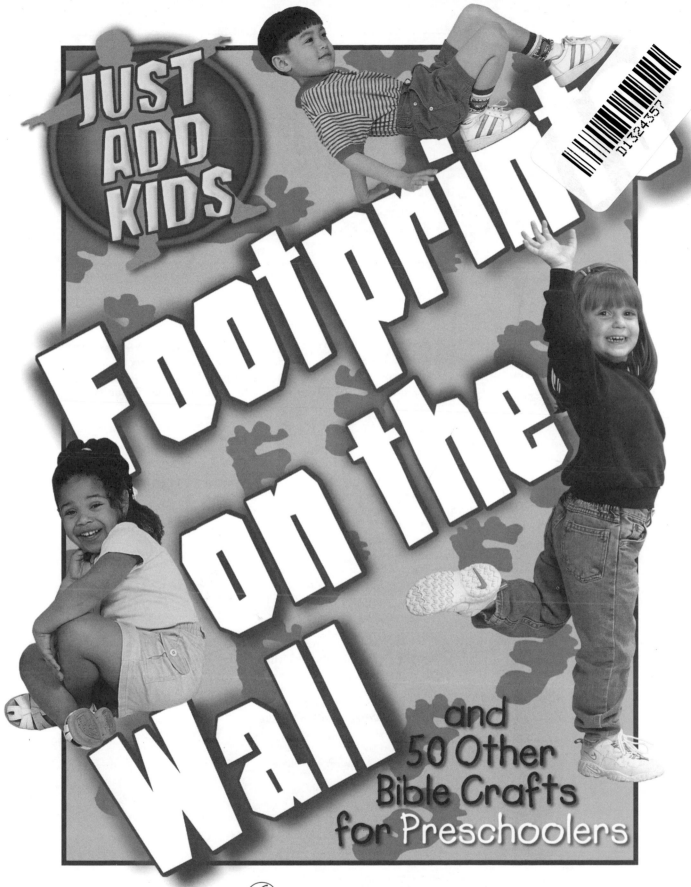

JUST ADD KIDS

Footprints on the Wall

and 50 Other Bible Crafts for Preschoolers

Abingdon Press

Nashville

Just Add Kids: Footprints on the Wall and 50 other Bible crafts for Preschoolers

ISBN 0-687-04850-8

Lead Editor: Daphna Flegal
Editor: Betsi H. Smith
Contributing Writer: Sharilyn S. Adair
Designed by: Paige Easter
Illustrated by: Robert S. Jones
Cover Photographs: Ron Benedict

00 01 02 03 04 05 06 07 08 09—10 9 8 7 6 5 4 3 2 1

MANUFACTURED IN THE UNITED STATES OF AMERICA

Preschool Crafts
Table of Contents

4

Introduction
Welcome to Just Add Kids

Who hasn't seen the child leaving class, proudly carrying his or her newly made creation? "Look what I made!" the child will say over and over until someone does stop and look and praise the child for such a fine creation. Sometimes it seems that craft time is the only classroom activity a child can remember, and there's a reason for that: Hands-on activity encourages learning.

Footprints on the Wall and 50 Other Bible Crafts for Preschoolers is loaded with crafts that your children will be proud to carry home. Many use reproducible pages, which are included here. And since each craft in *Footprints on the Wall* relates to a specific event in the Bible, your children are learning while they're creating.

Each child in your class is unique, with his or her own family background and experiences. But preschoolers do have some common traits. Understanding those traits will help you in your classroom:

- Preschoolers have lots of energy. They enjoy movement, although they are still struggling with fine motor skills.
- Preschoolers love anything silly, whether they're laughing, saying nonsense words, or singing a fun song. They are learning to identify colors and shapes.
- Preschoolers are just beginning to share. They are learning to interact, to respect others' feelings, and to wait until it's their turn. They may have a hard time leaving their parents.

For guidelines on how to make the most out of your crafts time, see the article on the next page. For other resources that will help you make your class time the best that it can be, don't miss the other books in the *Just Add Kids* collection:

- *Don't Get Wet Feet and 50 Other Bible Stories for Preschoolers.*
- *Ring 'Round Jericho and 50 Other Bible Games for Preschoolers.*
- *The Jailhouse Rocked and 50 Other Bible Stories for Elementary Children.*
- *Downright Upright and 50 Other Bible Games for Elementary Children.*
- *From Bags to Bushes and 50 Other Bible Crafts for Elementary Children.*

Using Crafts to Teach God's Word

Children learn through creating. Whether it's painting, cutting, coloring, gluing, or squishing clay through their fingers, children are perhaps most like God the Creator when they are creating.

Follow these simple guidelines to make craft time a success in your classroom.

- **Create a craft center.** If possible, set up your craft center in an uncarpeted area. While tables may be obstacles in other areas of your classroom, they work well here. Keep basic supplies on hand: glue, tape, construction paper, scissors (safety scissors, if you have young children), crayons, markers, and so forth.

- **Plan ahead.** Gather all the materials the children will need to complete their craft. Some crafts will require photocopying, cutting, and even some assembly. You will want to complete these steps before class begins. Make the craft ahead of time so that you understand the process and can help your children, if they need it.

- **Make it messy.** Some of the best crafts are the messiest ones. You may not want to have a messy craft every time you meet; but add them occasionally, and just watch the children enjoy themselves. It's wise to keep paint smocks on hand. (These can be as simple as adult-size shirts that the children wear over their clothes.) Also have hand-washing supplies available. Keep cloths nearby during craft time to mop up any spills.

- **Make cleanup time a part of craft time.** Children love to help, so use that to your advantage when it's time for cleanup. Give the children specific instructions: "Cathy, please put the crayons back in the box. Bryce, please put the scraps of paper in the trash can. Jana, please put all the chairs back around the table." Be sure to thank the children for their help.

- **Give lots of praise.** Talk with the children as they work. Look for and compliment anyone who is sharing the craft supplies. Find words of praise for each child as he or she creates. Remember, especially with young children, the process of creating is much more important than the finished product.

OLD TESTAMENT

God Created

craft

Supplies: tree trunk picture (see page 9), crayons or markers, green crepe paper, glue

Tree Tales

Photocopy the tree trunk picture (see page 9) for each child. Give each child a picture. Let the children decorate the tree trunk with crayons or markers.

Give each child a short strip of green crepe paper. Let the children tear the crepe paper into small pieces. Have the children glue the pieces onto their trees to make leaves.

    Say: God made our beautiful world. God made the sun and moon and stars. God made the plants and flowers and trees. God made the fish and birds and animals.

Have the children place their tree pictures on the floor in an open area of the room. Have the children stand beside their pictures.

    Say: God made the sun that shines on the trees. (*Make a circle with arms over head.*) God made the rain that waters the trees. (*Wiggle fingers up and down for raindrops.*) God made the wind that blows the leaves on the trees. (*Move arms in large, sweeping motions.*) God made the birds that nest in the trees. (*Move arms up and down like wings.*) God made the squirrels that play in the trees. (*Skip around pictures.*)

Bible
Genesis
1:1-25

God Created People

craft

Supplies: "Look at Me" page (see page 11), paint smocks, paper towels, shallow trays, tempera paint, pen, hand-washing supplies

Thumbody Special

Photocopy the "Look at Me" page (see page 11) for each child.

Say: God made people. (*Hold up a hand and wiggle your fingers.*) Each one of us has different fingerprints. Each person is special.

Have the children wear smocks. Place paper towels in shallow trays. Pour tempera paint on the paper towels to make paint pads.

Give each child a "Look at Me" page. Show the children how to press their thumbs and fingers onto the paint pads and then onto their papers to make thumbprints and fingerprints. Let the children make as many prints as they wish on their pages.

Read the poem at the top of the page to the children. Print each child's name in the space provided.

Say: God made (*child's name*). (*Child's name*) is special.

Have the children wash their hands. Set the fingerprints aside to dry.

© 1999 Abingdon Press.

Bible
Genesis
1:26-27

Look at me, look at me.
I am special 'cause God made me!

name

Noah's Ark

craft

Supplies: plastic margarine or whipped topping container with lid, water, liquid dishwashing soap, drinking straw, paper punch

Bubble, Bubble

Make a bubble machine for the children to enjoy when they learn about Noah and the ark.

Use a paper punch to punch two holes in the lid of a plastic margarine or whipped topping container. Pour about ½ cup water in the container and add about one tablespoon liquid dishwashing soap.

Place the lid on the container. Insert a straw into one of the holes. Show the children how to blow through the straw to make bubbles come out of the other hole.

© 1997 Abingdon Press.

Bible
Genesis
7:1-18

God's Promise to Abraham

craft

Supplies: tent picture (see page 14), green construction paper, scissors, knitting needle, cloth, craft sand, glue, craft sticks, star stickers

Desert Dwellings

Before class cut green construction paper into narrow strips about two inches long. Crumple them or roll them around a knitting needle. Cut cloth into small scraps. Set the craft sand, cloth scraps, and construction paper on a work table. Give each child a copy of the picture of the tent in the desert (see page 14) and a craft stick.

Say: Abraham was a man who traveled and lived in the desert because God told him to leave his old home and go to a new place. The new place was a special land called Palestine. Let's make desert pictures.

For each child pour four puddles of glue: one on the ground area, one on the tent, and one on the leafy area of each of the two palm trees. Pour one puddle at a time. Have the children spread the glue with their craft sticks.

Encourage each child to sprinkle sand over the ground area, to glue cloth scraps to the tent, and to glue crumpled construction paper to the palm trees. As you pour the glue, alternate the areas among the children so that at any time some children are adding sand, some are adding cloth scraps, and some are adding leaves to their pictures.

Let the children enjoy gluing the different textures to their pictures. Do not insist that they put the items in exact places.

Say: God said that Abraham would have as many grandchildren as there are stars. Let's add stars to our pictures.

Let the children add star stickers to the skies of their pictures. Set the pictures aside to dry.

Say: God was with Abraham as he traveled and lived in the desert.

Bible
Genesis
12:1–9

© 2000 Abingdon Press.

Abraham and Sarah

craft

Supplies: tent pattern (see page 16), black or brown yarn, scissors, glue, craft sticks

A Hairy Home

Before class cut black or brown yarn into fine pieces with sharp scissors to make yarn fuzz. Make a copy of the tent pattern (see page 16) for each child.

Although the children will glue yarn on the pattern as it is lying flat, you should crease the folds ahead of time in order to know where they are when the pattern is covered with yarn. Fold all the solid lines in one direction, folding the paper away from you to make outside creases. Fold the dotted lines in the opposite direction, so that the folds go inside the roof of the tent.

Put the yarn fuzz and glue bottles in the center of the table. Give each child a copy of the tent pattern and a craft stick.

Say: Abraham and Sarah were people who lived long ago in Bible times. They lived in the desert in a special kind of tent made from the hair of goats. When the goats' hair got very long, Abraham's workers cut it off to help the goats keep cool. Then other workers made the hair into yarn and made tents from the yarn. The tents were dark brown or black, and they kept rain out and also were cool inside when the sun was hot. Let's make tents like Abraham and Sarah's.

Let the children pour their own glue onto the side of the paper with lines on it. Encourage them to spread the glue around with their craft sticks until a thin layer covers their papers.

Have the children cover their papers with yarn fuzz. Set the papers aside to dry. When they are dry, you will have to recrease the folds in order for the tents to stand up.

Bible
Genesis
18:1-6

Say: God was with Abraham and Sarah when they lived in their tent in the desert.

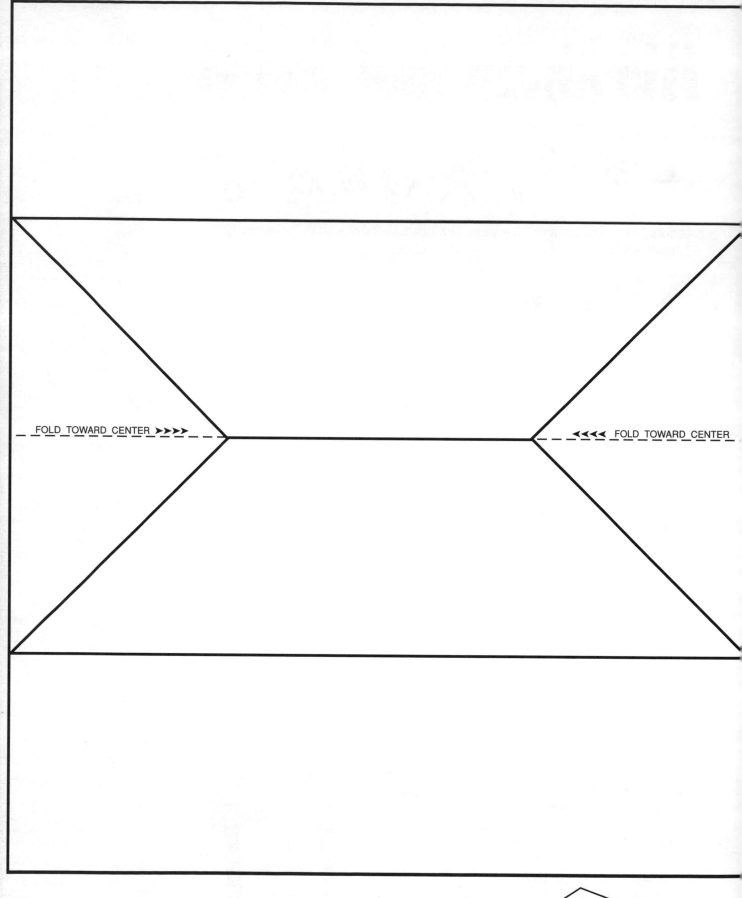

FOLD TOWARD CENTER ▶▶▶▶   ◀◀◀◀ FOLD TOWARD CENTER

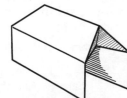

Rebekah and Isaac

craft

Supplies: construction paper, scissors, several colors of tissue paper, white glue, water, shallow bowl, paintbrushes, tape (optional: blow dryer or microwave)

Bangle Bracelets

Before class cut construction paper into strips thin enough and long enough to go around each child's wrist. Each child should have a bracelet strip. Cut several colors of tissue paper into 3- to 4-inch squares.

Make a mixture of half white glue and half water in a shallow bowl. Put the glue mixture, paintbrushes, scissors, and tissue paper in the center of the table. Give each child a bracelet strip.

Say: When Rebekah watered camels for a visitor, he gave her some bracelets. Let's make bracelets like Rebekah's.

Invite the children to cut or tear the tissue paper into small pieces. Then show them how to paint their bracelet strips with the glue mixture and how to lay pieces of tissue paper on them to make pretty colors. Put the bracelet strips aside to dry.

When each bracelet is dry, tape the ends together to form a circular band.

Hint: If you have a helper, the bracelets can be dried with a hair dryer or put into the church microwave for about three minutes for faster drying. When the bracelets are dry, let the children enjoy wearing them.

Say: Rebekah was a woman in Bible times who trusted God. She knew that God was always with her.

Bible
Genesis 24:1-4,
10-34, 34-44, 50-59

Jacob's Ladder

craft

Supplies: plain paper, crayons, stapler and staples, newspapers or recycled paper, tape

Rock Pillows

Say: Today we're talking about a man named Jacob. One day Jacob was going to another city. He traveled all day long. When it was night, Jacob stopped. He found a rock to use as a pillow and went to sleep. Let's make our papers into pretend rocks.

Give each child two pieces of plain paper. Show the children how to crumple the paper into a ball and then smooth the paper flat again. Have the children repeat this process several times.

Say: Rocks are hard and rough. Feel the crumples you have made in your papers. (*Have the children run their fingers over their crumpled papers.*) Let's pretend that the crumples are the rough edges of our rocks.

Have the children place their papers flat on the table. Let the children color their papers with crayons. When each child has finished coloring, stack the two papers together, decorated side out. Staple around three sides of the papers, leaving one side open.

Place a stack of newspapers or other recycled paper on the table or floor. Show the children how to tear off sheets of newspaper and crumple them into balls. Have the children stuff the newspaper balls into their pillows. When each pillow is stuffed, staple the fourth side closed. Cover the prongs of the staples with strips of tape.

Say: While Jacob was sleeping, he had a dream. God spoke to Jacob in the dream. "God said, 'Remember, I will be with you'" (Genesis 28:15, *Good News Bible*, adapted).

Bible
Genesis
28:10-22

Joseph and His Brothers

craft

Supplies: grocery-size paper bags, scissors, crayons

Bag It

Cut a paper bag into a coat for each child. Turn the bag upside down. Cut a slit up the middle of one side. At the top of the slit, continue to cut and form a circular space for the neck.

Cut holes for the arms on the two narrow sides of the bag. If the bags have printing on them, turn them inside out.

Say: The Bible story tells a story about a young man named Joseph. Joseph's father gave Joseph a very special robe. The robe had long sleeves and many colors. Let's make Joseph's robe.

Encourage the children to decorate the paper bag robes with many colors of crayons. Help the children put on their robes.

Say: Joseph grew up and had many adventures in a place called Egypt. As Joseph grew, he remembered that God was with him. God is always with us.

Bible
Genesis
37:12–33

19

Baby Moses

Craft 1

Supplies: grocery-size brown paper bag, masking tape

Sack—It Basket

Fold the top half of a brown paper grocery bag down inside the bag. Fold the top half of the bag down inside the bag once again. This will make the basket about 4½ inches deep.

Let the children add masking tape strips to the outside of the basket. Tear masking tape into short strips. Lightly tape one end of the strips to the table. Let the children pull up the strips and tape them onto the bag.

Say: The Bible tells a story about baby Moses and his family. Baby Moses' mother made a basket for baby Moses. She put baby Moses in the basket to keep him safe. Baby Moses' sister watched over baby Moses. God planned for the baby to have a loving mother and a loving sister, just as God planned for your family to love you.

© 1998 Abingdon Press.

Bible
Exodus
2:1–10

craft 2

Supplies: baby in a blanket and baby face (see pages 22 and 23), glue, scissors, stapler and staples, cotton balls or tissues, baby basket (see craft on previous page)

Oh, Baby!

Photocopy and cut out two copies of the baby-in-a-blanket figure (see page 22). Photocopy and cut out one copy of the baby face (see page 23).

Choose one of the blanket figures to be the front of baby Moses. Glue the face onto the blanket figure. The second blanket figure will make the back of baby Moses.

Place the two figures together so that the face shows on the front and the blanket shows on the back. Staple around the edges, leaving a 4-inch opening. Let the children work together to stuff the figure with cotton balls or tissues. Staple the opening together.

> **Say:** Today we're talking about baby Moses and his family. Moses' mother placed baby Moses in a basket. She cared about Moses and wanted to keep him safe.

Place the baby Moses figure in the grocery bag basket (see "Sack-It Basket" on the previous page). Choose one child to hide his or her eyes, or have the child leave the room with another teacher. Hide the baby and basket somewhere in the room.

Have the child uncover his or her eyes, or return to the room. Let the child look around the room for baby Moses in the basket.

When the child is moving near the basket, have the other children shout, "Oh, baby!" When the child moves away from the basket, have the children whisper, "Oh, baby!"

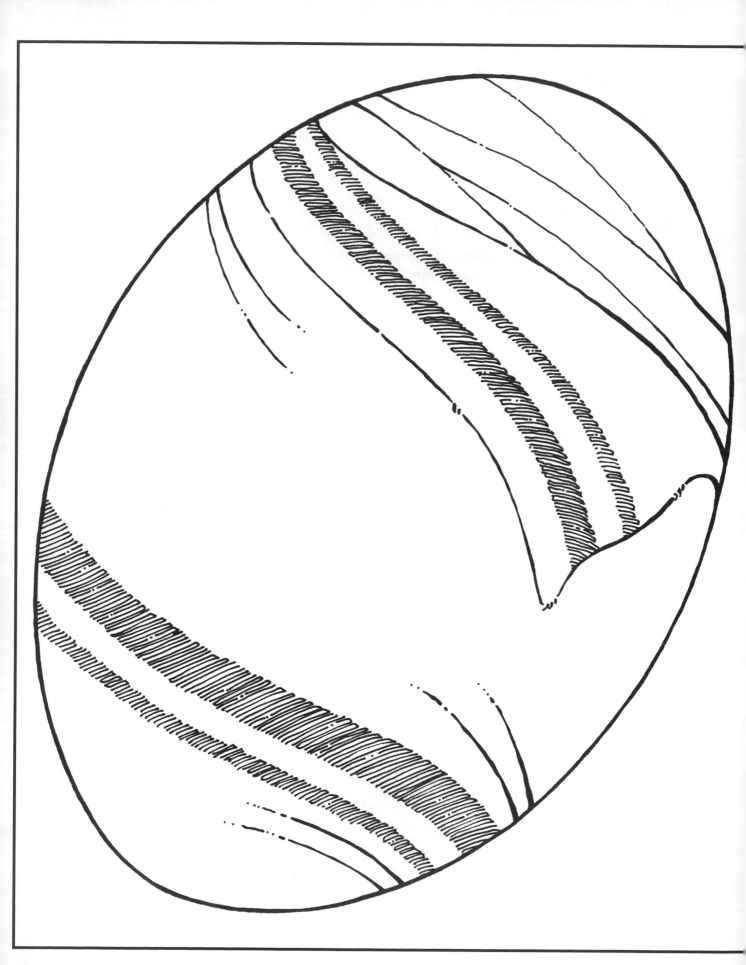

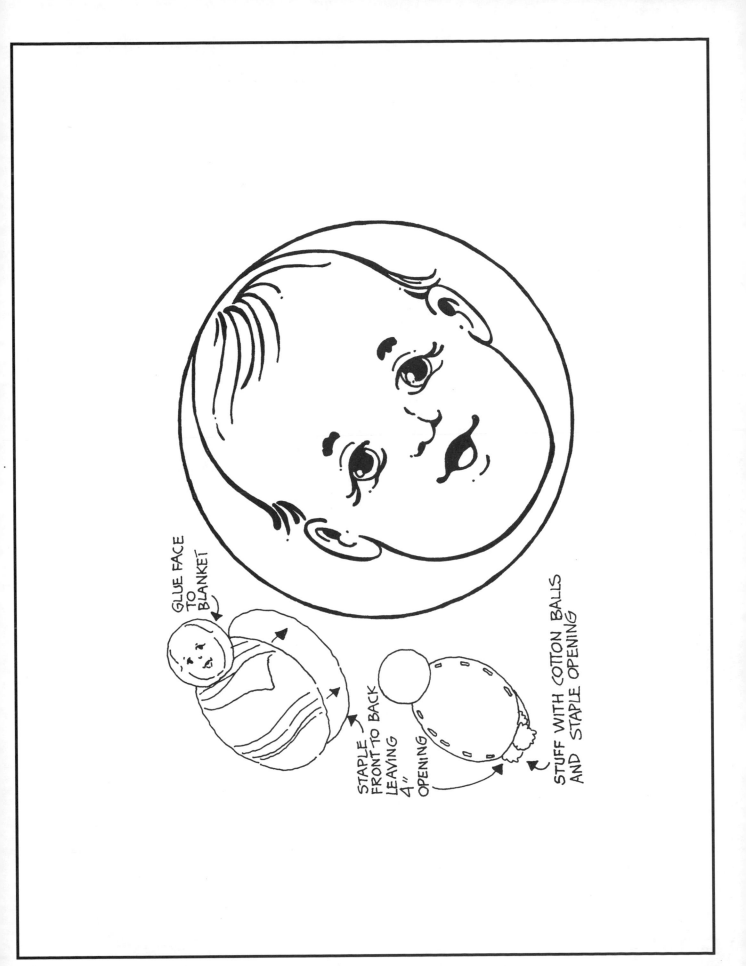

GLUE FACE TO BLANKET

STAPLE FRONT TO BACK LEAVING 4" OPENING

STUFF WITH COTTON BALLS AND STAPLE OPENING

Let My People Go!

craft

Supplies: Moses and Hebrew people puppets (see pages 25 and 26); crayons; glue, tape, or stapler and staples

Puppet Parade

Make one photocopy of the Moses puppet (see page 25). Photocopy the Hebrew people puppet (see page 26) for each child. Give each child a Hebrew people puppet. Let the children decorate the puppets with crayons. You may want the children to work together to decorate the Moses puppet, or leave the puppet as it is.

Say: Today we're talking about a man named Moses (*Show the Moses puppet.*) and the Hebrew people. (*Show the Hebrew people puppet.*) God wanted Moses to lead the Hebrew people out of Egypt. Moses trusted God.

Help the children fold their Hebrew people puppets along the dotted lines. Have the children glue, tape, or staple the sides of the puppets together. Show the children how to place their hands inside the bottom openings of the puppets.

Fold the Moses puppet along the dotted line. Glue, tape, or staple the sides of the puppet together. Put your hand inside the Moses puppet.

Say: God wanted Moses to lead the Hebrew people out of Egypt. Let's pretend that I am Moses (*Hold up the Moses puppet.*) and that you are the Hebrew people. Hebrew people, let me see your puppets. Follow me as I lead you out of Egypt.

Lead the children around the room. Go in circles around tables and chairs, go out your doorway, wander up and down a hallway, go back in your doorway, and crawl under a table. Have a good time with the parade, but always keep safety in mind.

© 1998 Abingdon Press.

Bible
Exodus
12:31-32; 37-39

24

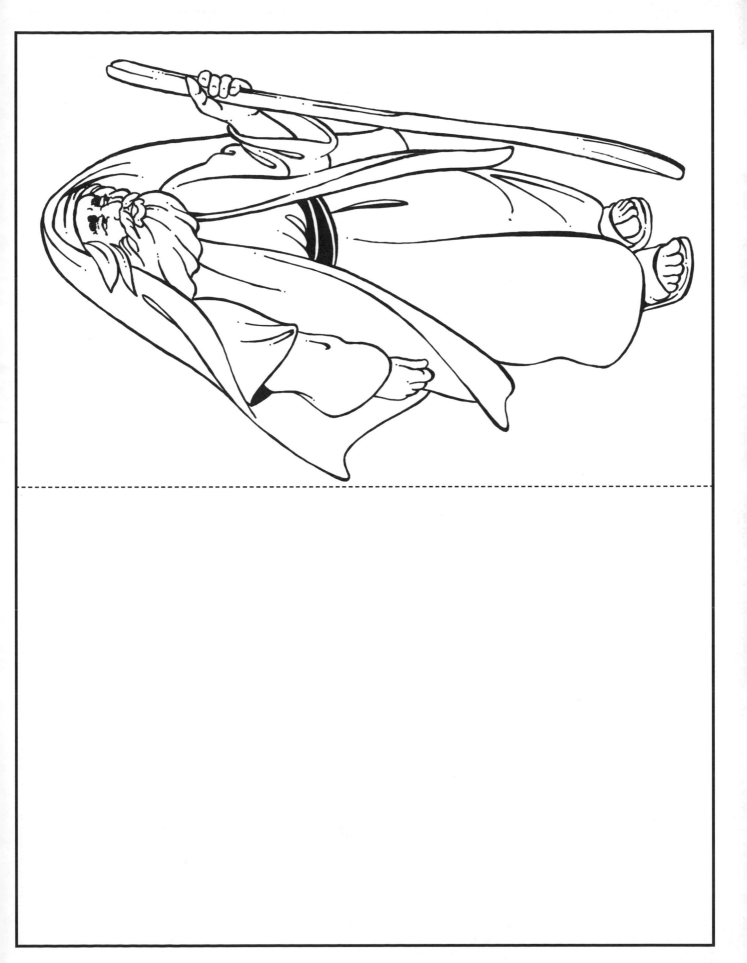

25

The Red Sea

craft

Supplies: paint smocks, shaving cream, sponges, hand-washing supplies (optional: plastic garbage bag)

Part the Waters

Have the children wear smocks to protect their clothing. Have them sit at a table. Squirt a small amount of shaving cream directly onto the table in front of each child. Let the children enjoy fingerpainting with the shaving cream.

> **Say:** God wanted Moses to lead the Hebrew people out of Egypt. Moses trusted God. He led the people out of Egypt across the Red Sea! Let's pretend that our shaving cream is the Red Sea.

Encourage the children to make a path through the shaving cream and "part the waters." When the children are finished, have them use sponges to wipe off the table. The shaving cream will leave the table clean.

If your situation allows, take the children outside for this activity. Place a plastic garbage bag on the grass. Have the children take off their shoes and socks. Squirt shaving cream on the plastic bag.

Make a path through the shaving cream and let the children walk through the Red Sea. Pick up the trash bag and throw it away. Wash hands and feet before going back inside.

© 1998 Abingdon Press.

Bible
Exodus
14:15-22

In the Wilderness

craft

Supplies: quail hats (see page 29), scissors, crayons, tape or stapler and staples, glue

Bird Bonnets

Photocopy and cut out the quail hats (see page 29) for each child. Give each child the quail section of the hat. Let the children decorate the hats with crayons.

Help each child tape or staple a headband strip to each side of the quail section. Measure the strips around the child's head. Glue or tape the ends of the strips together so that the hat fits around the child's head.

Say: Moses led the Hebrew people out of Egypt into the wilderness. When the people were in the wilderness, they needed food to eat. God gave the people food.

Encourage the children to wear their quail hats.

Say: God planned for the Hebrew people to have quail to eat. Quail is a kind of bird that people ate, just like we eat chicken.

Bible
Exodus
16:11-15

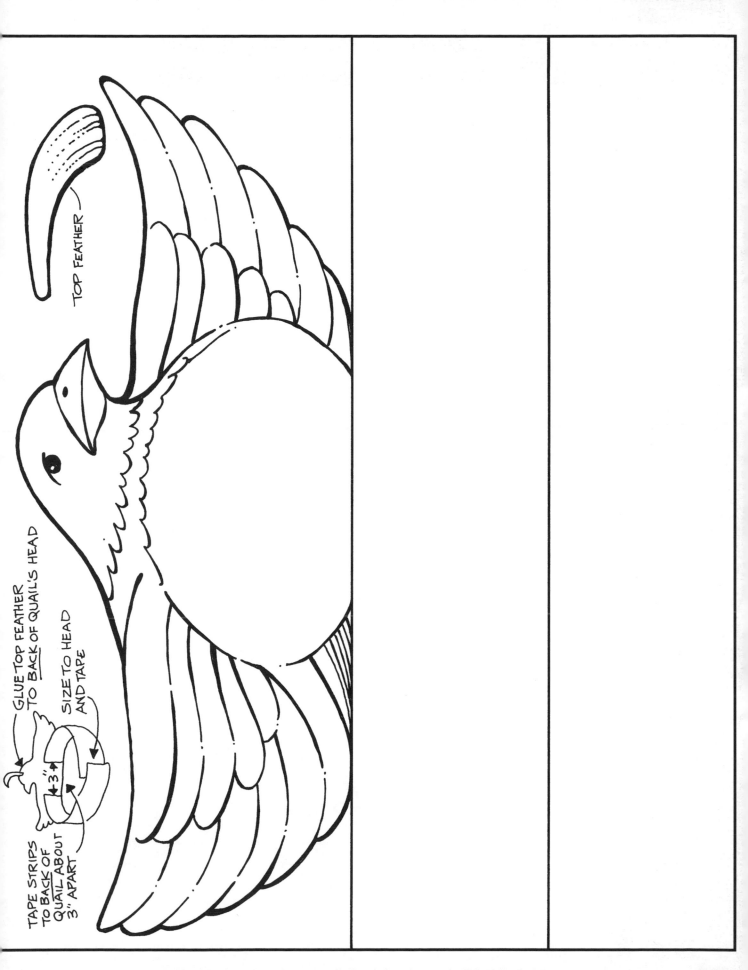

TOP FEATHER

GLUE TOP FEATHER TO BACK OF QUAIL'S HEAD

SIZE TO HEAD AND TAPE

TAPE STRIPS TO BACK OF QUAIL ABOUT 3" APART

3"

Joshua and the Battle of Jericho

craft

Supplies: paper horns (see page 31), crayons, tape

Trumpet Tunes

Photocopy the paper horns (see page 31) for each child. Let the children decorate the paper horns with crayons.

Help the children roll their papers into a horn shape. Tape the edges together. Show the children how to hold their horns up to their mouths and pretend to blow.

Say: God wanted Joshua to take the people into the city of Jericho, but there was a big wall around the city to keep Joshua and the people out. God told Joshua to have the people march around the walls. Seven men led the people around the walls. The men blew on trumpets as they marched. Joshua trusted God and did what God wanted him to do.

© 1997 Abingdon Press.

Bible
Joshua
6:1-20

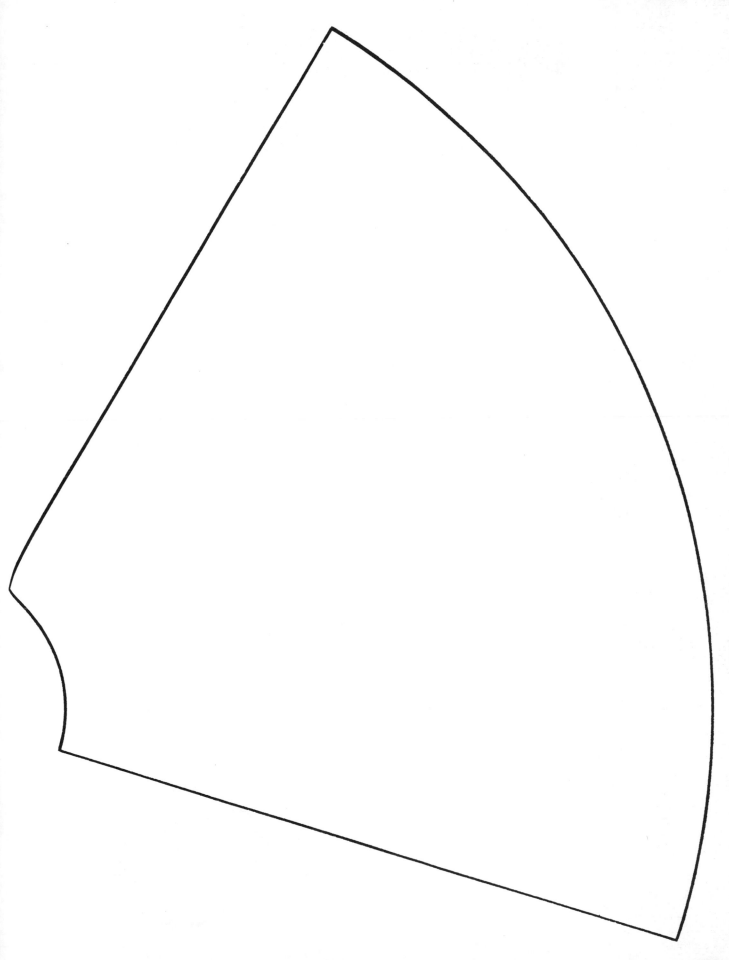

Ruth

craft

Supplies: grain picture (see page 33); newspaper, crayons, baby oil, cotton balls; or cotton swabs, shallow tray or box lid, birdseed, glue

Picture This

Photocopy the grain picture (see page 33) for each child. Give each child a picture. Let the children make stained-glass windows or seed mosaics with their pictures.

Stained-glass windows: Cover the work area with newspapers. Let the children color the pictures with crayons. Have the children turn the pictures over. Pour a small amount of baby oil on a cotton ball. Show the children how to rub the oil over the backs of their pictures. Hold the pictures up to the light. The oil will make the pictures translucent.

Seed mosaics: Have the children use cotton swabs to brush glue onto their pictures. Place each picture in a shallow tray or box lid. Show the children how to sprinkle birdseed over the glue. Shake off the excess seeds.

Say: Today we're talking about a woman named Ruth. Ruth was kind to her mother-in-law, Naomi. Ruth left her home and went with Naomi to a town called Bethlehem. When they got to Bethlehem, Ruth went to the fields to find grain so that she and Naomi would be able to make bread to eat. While Ruth was picking up the grain, she met a kind man named Boaz. Ruth and Boaz got married. God was with Ruth and Naomi and Boaz. God is always with us.

© 1998 Abingdon Press.

Bible
Ruth
1–4

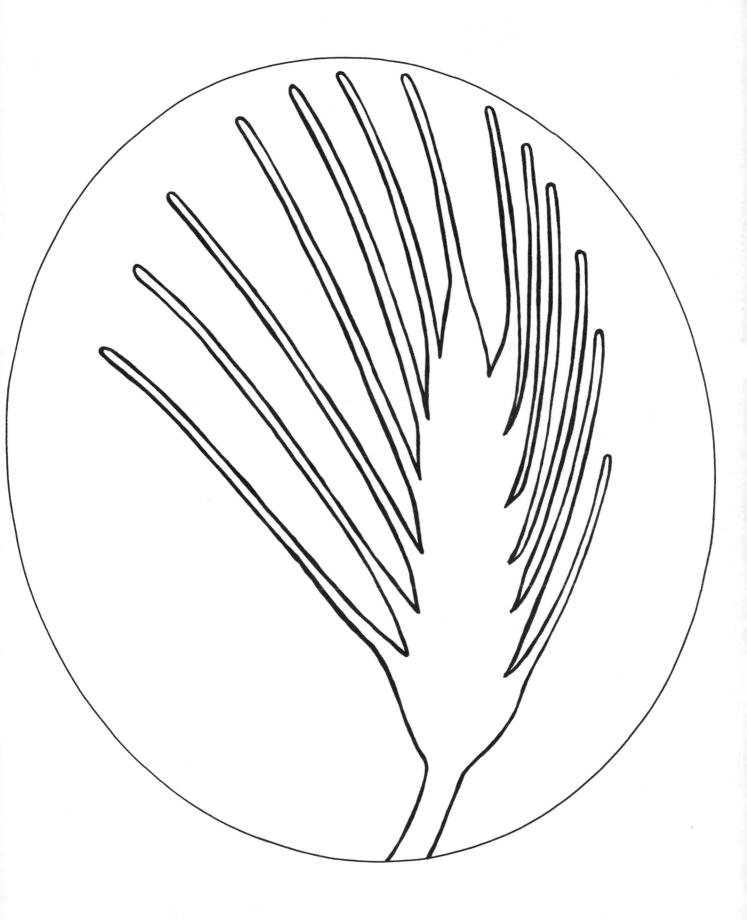

God Calls Samuel

craft

Supplies: Samuel puppet pop-up (see page 35), crayons, glue or tape, craft sticks

Puppet Pop—Ups

Photocopy and cut out the Samuel puppet pop-up (see page 35) for each child. Let the children decorate the puppet pieces with crayons.

Say: The Bible tells a story about a boy named Samuel. Samuel grew from a baby to a boy. God was with Samuel as he grew.

Show each child how to fold the mat along the dotted lines. Glue or tape the sides of the mats together. Leave the top and bottom edges of the mats open.

Help the children glue or tape their Samuel figures onto craft sticks. Show each child how to slide the Samuel puppet into the the pocket formed by the mat.

Say: Let's say the Bible verse together. ("*As Samuel grew up, the LORD was with him.*" — *1 Samuel 3:19*) I will say the first part of the verse. When you hear me say "up," push your Samuel puppet up out of the sleeping mat and say the second part of the verse, "the Lord was with him."

Say the first part of the verse with the children. Have the children push up their puppets and say the second part of the verse. Repeat the verse several times.

© 1998 Abingdon Press.

Bible
1 Samuel
3:1–10

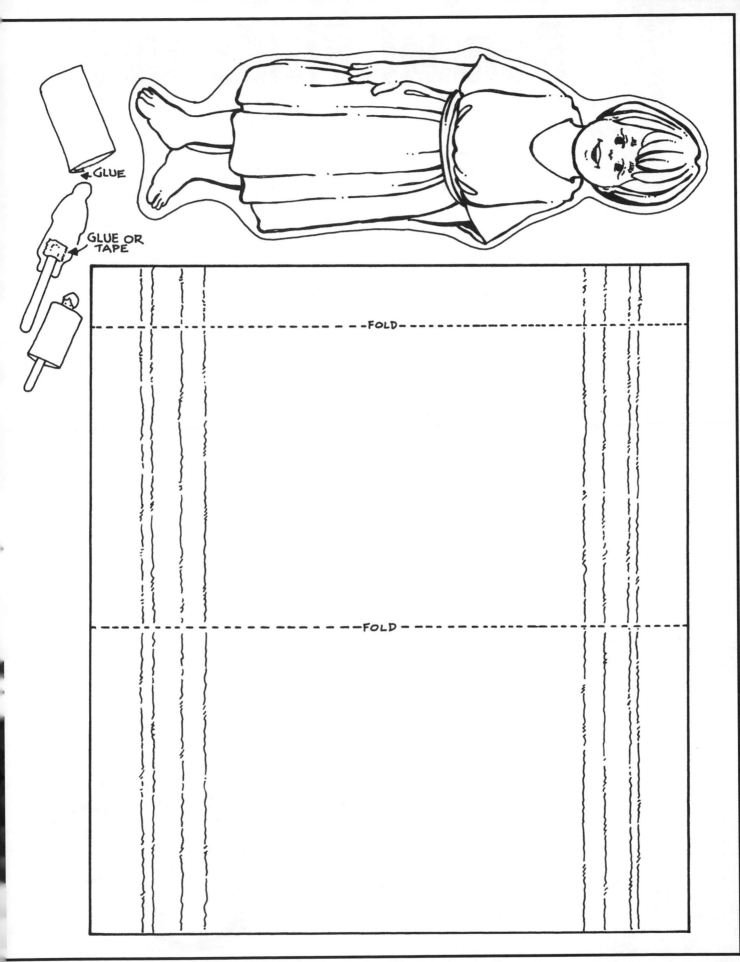

GLUE

GLUE OR
TAPE

FOLD

FOLD

Samuel Finds David

craft

Supplies: heart crown (see page 37), crayons; glue, tape, or stapler and staples; large basket or bag

Crown o' Hearts

Photocopy and cut out the heart crown (see page 37) for each child. Give each child the heart piece. Let the children color the heart pieces with crayons.

Say: Today we're talking about Samuel and David. Samuel grew into a man. When he was a man, God sent him to find a new king. God had Samuel choose a young boy named David to be the new king. God chose David because God knew David had a loving heart. That meant that David loved God and others.

Help each child glue, tape, or staple the ends of the crown pieces together to make one long strip. If you use staples, make sure the prongs of the staples are facing outward, away from the child's head.

Write the child's name on the strip. Measure the crown strip around each child's head. Tape, glue, or staple the ends of the crown strip together. Have the children place their crowns in a large basket or bag.

Have the children move to one side of the room. Bring the heart crowns and move to the opposite side of the room. Pick up one of the crowns from the basket or bag. Notice the child's name.

Say: I am looking for someone with a happy smile and a loving heart. I choose (*child's name*). (*Child's name*), hop to me.

Have the child hop across the room to you. Place the crown on the child's head.

Say: (*Child's name*) has a loving heart. (*Child's name*) loves God and others.

Continue until every child has moved across the room and received his or her crown. Vary how you tell each child to move (march, gallop, crawl, jump, walk on tiptoe, walk with giant steps, walk with baby steps).

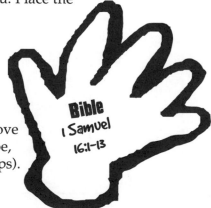

Bible
1 Samuel
16:1-13

David and Jonathan

craft

Supplies: newspaper, paint smocks, paper towels, plastic containers, water, paintbrushes, black nonpermanent marker

Hearts

Cover the work area with newspapers and have the children wear paint smocks to protect their clothing. Give each child a section of paper towel. Pour water into plastic containers and give each child a paintbrush.

Use a black nonpermanent marker to draw a large heart on the paper towels. Show the children how to quickly dip their brushes into the water and paint over the marker. The marker will begin to run and bleed onto the paper towel.

Use this activity whenever you talk about David and Jonathan and their friendship. The hearts can help the children remember that David and Jonathan loved each other and that God loved them, just like God loves us.

© 1997 Abingdon Press.

Bible
1 Samuel
18:1-4

Abigail

craft

Supplies: dove picture (see page 40), newspaper, paint smocks, flour, water, salt, large bowl, white liquid tempera paint, plastic squeeze bottles

Peace Painting

Let the children make puffy paint. Cover the table with newspapers and have the children wear paint smocks to protect their clothing.

Mix equal parts flour, salt, and water in a large bowl. Add white liquid tempera paint to color the mixture. Pour the paint into plastic squeeze bottles.

Photocopy the dove picture (see page 40) for each child. Let the children squeeze the puffy paint onto their pictures to decorate their doves.

Say: Sometimes we use pictures of doves to remind us of peace. The Bible tells the story of a woman named Abigail. Abigail worked for peace. She helped stop a fight.

Bible
I Samuel
25:2-43

39

Solomon's Temple

Craft 1

Supplies: Solomon's Temple picture (see page 43), crayons or markers, glue, craft sticks, flat tray, gold glitter, paper

House of God, House of Gold

Put crayons or markers on the table. Give each child a copy of the picture of Solomon's Temple (see page 43). Invite the children to color the pictures.

> **Say:** King Solomon lived long ago in Bible times. King Solomon built a beautiful Temple. The Temple was a special place where people could worship and praise God.

> **Say:** The Temple was built of white stone. Some of the stones were covered in shiny gold.

Pour a puddle of glue on each child's picture. Encourage the children to use their craft sticks to spread the glue. Let each child in turn place her or his picture in a flat tray and sprinkle gold glitter over it.

Have the child shake off extra glitter into the tray. Retrieve the extra glitter by pouring it from the tray onto a sheet of paper with a crease down the middle. Tap the paper to direct the glitter into the crease, and pour the glitter back into the container.

© 2000 Abingdon Press.

Bible
1 Kings
6:1-38

craft 2

Supplies: crown and crown strip (see page 44), paper-backed foil such as Christmas wrapping paper or colored construction paper, scissors, crayons or markers, glue sticks, large sequins, masking tape, clear tape

Solomon's Crown

Before class cut diamond shapes, circles, and ovals from paper-backed foil such as Christmas wrapping paper or from colored construction paper.

Photocopy and cut out the crown and crown strip (see page 44) for each child.

Distribute the crown sections to the children. Put crayons or markers, glue sticks, the "jewels" you cut from paper, and large sequins in the center of the table.

   Say: King Solomon was a king who lived long ago in Bible times. Kings wear crowns on their heads. Let's make King Solomon's crown.

Invite the children to color their crowns and to glue foil jewels and sequins on them with glue sticks. When each child is ready, use clear tape to put the two pieces of the child's crown together and fit it to the child's head.

Remove the crown and put a long strip of masking tape around the inside of the crown to strengthen it.

43

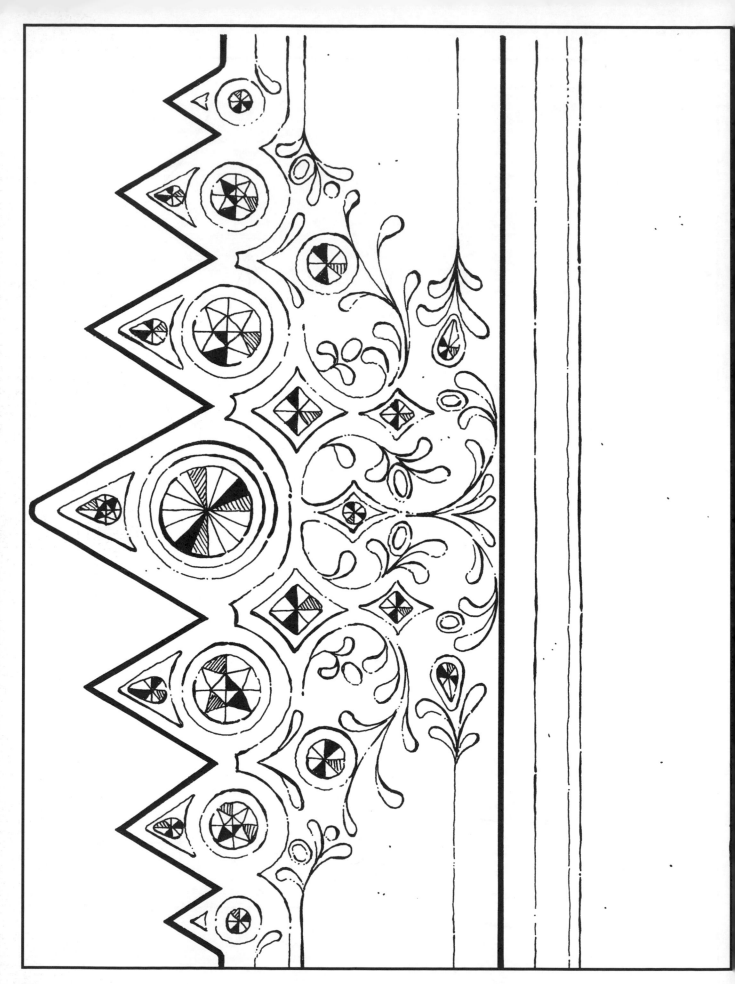

44

Josiah

craft

Supplies: clay jar (see page 46), tape, sandpaper or corrugated cardboard, crayons with papers removed, brown paper bags, scissors

Potter's Corner

Photocopy the clay jar (see page 46) for each child. Tape a piece of sandpaper or corrugated cardboard to the table.

Lightly tape each clay jar picture over the sandpaper or cardboard. Let the children make texture rubbings by rubbing crayons (with papers removed) over their jar pictures. The texture will show through the rubbing.

Help each child fold his or her jar picture in half along the dotted line. Then help each child roll the strip into a tube and tape the edges to make a three-dimensional jar.

Cut a 5-by-7-inch rectangle out of a brown paper bag for each child. Let the children decorate the papers with crayons. Show the children how to roll the papers like a scroll and place them inside their jars.

Say: King Josiah was faithful. He found a very important scroll. The scroll told the people how to be faithful and how to do what God wanted them to do. The scroll was inside a clay jar.

Bible
2 Kings
22:3–23:3

45

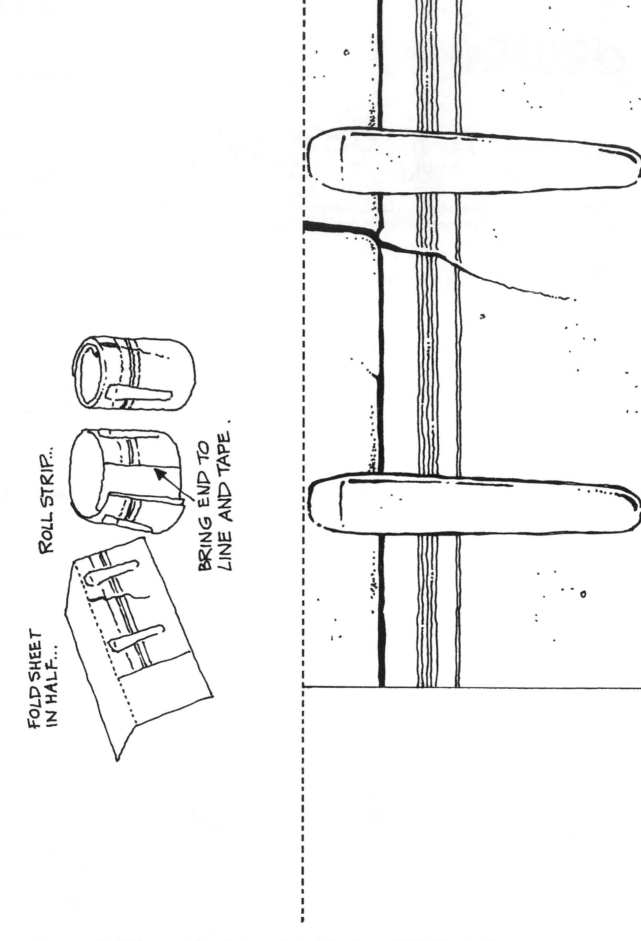

FOLD SHEET IN HALF...

ROLL STRIP...

BRING END TO LINE AND TAPE.

Esther

craft

Supplies: colored drinking straws, scissors, yarn, tape

Jazzy Jewels

Cut colored drinking straws into one-inch pieces. Or let the children use safety scissors to cut the drinking straws into small pieces. Cutting drinking straws can be a successful cutting experience for young children.

Cut yarn into 36-inch lengths. Wrap one end of each length of yarn with tape to make the yarn easier to thread through the straw pieces.

   Say: The Bible tells a story about a woman named Esther. Esther became queen. Let's make jewelry for kings and queens.

Let the children make necklaces by stringing the straw pieces onto the yarn. Encourage the children to wear their necklaces.

   Say: Queen Esther was very brave. She helped her people.

Bible
Esther
2:16-17; 7:1-6;
8:3-8

Bible—Times Shepherds

craft

Supplies: sheep (see page 49); scissors, crayons or markers; tape, glue, or stapler and staples; cotton balls; yarn

Stuffed Sheep

Photocopy and cut out two copies of the sheep (see page 49) for each child. Give each child the two copies.

Say: Shepherds take care of sheep. People in a country called Guatemala make cloth animals called *animalitos*. Let's make a sheep *animalito*.

Help each child place the sheep cutouts together so that the cutouts are nose to nose. Use a crayon or marker to make a dot for the eye on each sheep.

Let the children use crayons or markers to decorate the side of the sheep with the eye dots.

Help each child place the two sheep pieces together so that the decorated sides face out. Staple, glue, or tape the edges of the sheep together, leaving an opening along the sheep's back.

Show the children how to stuff the sheep with cotton balls. Staple, glue, or tape the opening closed. Let the children glue on strips of yarn for the sheep's tail.

© 1998 Abingdon Press.

Bible
Psalm 23

48

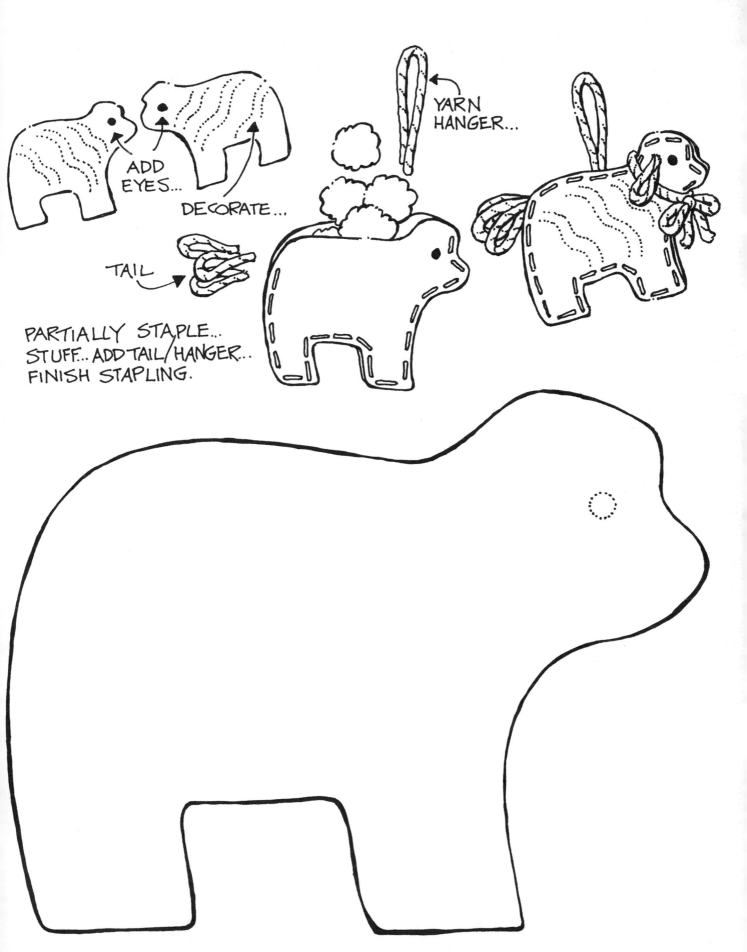

ADD EYES...

DECORATE...

TAIL

YARN HANGER...

PARTIALLY STAPLE...
STUFF...ADD TAIL/HANGER...
FINISH STAPLING.

Bible—Times Potters

Use these recipes when you are talking about potters fashioning things from clay, or just whenever you want the children to enjoy manipulating clay.

craft 1

Supplies: flour, salt, salad oil, cream of tartar, water, food coloring, wooden spoon, airtight container

Cooked Play Dough

Mix 2 cups flour, 1 cup salt, and 2 tablespoons cream of tartar in a saucepan. Add food coloring to 4 cups water and add to the flour mixture. Add two tablespoons salad oil and mix well. Cook over low heat, stirring constantly with a wooden spoon. When the mixture is too heavy to move around, turn it out onto a flat surface and knead it as soon as it is cool enough to touch. Keep in an airtight container.

© 1998 Abingdon Press.

craft 2

Supplies: flour, salt, cooking oil, water, alum, mixing bowl, airtight container, spoon

No—Cook Play Dough

Mix 1½ cups salt, 4 cups flour, and 1 teaspoon alum together in a plastic bowl. Add 1 cup water and ½ cup cooking oil.When the dough forms a ball around the spoon, knead it well, adding water if it is too crumbly.

Store in an airtight container. This dough is easy to manipulate and is good for younger children.

Bible
Jeremiah 18:1-6

© 1998 Abingdon Press.

Daniel and the Lions

craft

Supplies: lion face (see page 52), crayons, small paper plates, glue, safety scissors, tape, craft sticks

Face a Lion

Cut out a lion face (see page 52) for each child. Let the children color the lion faces with crayons. Give each child a small paper plate. Have the children glue the lion face in the middle of the paper plate.

Give each child a pair of safety scissors. Show the children how to use the scissors to make cuts around the edges of the paper plates. This will make the lion's mane. Remember that young children are learning to use scissors. They need to practice their cutting skills. Affirm their efforts.

Glue or tape the paper plates onto craft sticks to make puppets.

Bible
Daniel
6:10–26

The Lord's Prayer

craft

Supplies: 3-by-5 cards or paper and scissors, stickers, paper plates, stapler and staples, crayons or markers

Prayer Pockets

Help each child in your class name people that he or she can pray for. Write the names on 3-by-5 cards or pieces of paper cut into 3-by-5-inch rectangles. Let the children decorate their cards with stickers.

Use two paper plates to make a prayer pocket for each child. Cut one paper plate in half. Place the paper plate half on top of the whole paper plate to form a pocket. Staple the plates together around the edges. Let the children decorate their paper plate pockets with crayons or markers.

Place the children's name cards inside their pockets.

Say: Jesus taught his friends about prayer. Each day you can pick a name card from the pocket and pray for that person.

Bible
Matthew
6:9-13

Peter's Mother—in—law

craft

Supplies: get-well card (see page 56), crayons or markers, glue, shallow tray or box lid, glitter

Get—Well Glitter

Photocopy the get-well card (see page 56) for each child. Give each child a card. Let the children color the inside of the cards.

> **Say:** Today we're talking about the day when Jesus healed Peter's mother-in-law. Jesus cared about people who were sick. We can care for people who are sick. One way we can care for people who are sick is to send them get-well cards.

Show the children how to fold the cards in half. Have the children place the cards so that the blank cover is facing up. Let the children spread glue over the covers. Have each child place the card in a shallow tray or box lid.

Show the children how to sprinkle glitter over the glue. Shake off the excess glitter into the shallow tray or box lid. Pour the excess glitter back into the glitter container to reuse. Set the cards aside to dry.

Make plans to send the cards to persons in your church who are sick. Check with your pastor or church secretary for names. Be sure to follow through and send the cards.

> **Say:** We will send our cards to (*name the people who will receive the cards*). Our cards will help (*name the people who will receive the cards*) feel better.

Bible
Matthew
8:14-15

Get Well Soon!

Matthew

craft

Supplies: money bag (see page 58), scissors, crayons, resealable plastic bag or lunch-size paper bag, glue

Money Bags

Photocopy the money bag (see page 58) for each child. Cut the money bags out along the circle. Give each child a bag. Let the children decorate the bags with crayons.

Give each child a resealable plastic bag or a lunch-size paper bag. Have the children glue the money bags onto the front of the bags.

Say: Matthew was a tax collector. A tax collector was someone who took money from people and gave it to the king. Most tax collectors cheated and kept some of the money for themselves. Nobody liked tax collectors, and nobody liked Matthew. One day Matthew met Jesus. Jesus asked Matthew to follow him. Matthew became one of the friends of Jesus.

Bible
Matthew
9:9

The Lost Sheep

craft

Supplies: sheep face, mouth, and ears (see page 60); scissors; cotton balls; lunch-size paper bags; glue

Fluffy Puppet

Before class photocopy and cut out the sheep face, mouth, and ears (see page 60) for each child. Cut cotton balls in half. Give each child a lunch-size paper bag and a copy of the sheep face, mouth, and ears. Place the glue and cotton ball halves in the center of the table.

Say: Jesus told a story about a shepherd who cared for his sheep. Let's make sheep.

Show each child how to glue the sheep's mouth under the bottom flap of the paper bag. Help the child glue the sheep's face on top of the bottom flap of the paper bag. Let her or him glue the ears on either side of the face. Let the children glue cotton ball halves on the sheep's face. Show the children how to place their hands inside the paper bags to make the puppets' mouths talk.

Say: Let's pretend that we are little sheep. Let your sheep puppets do what mine does.

Munch! Munch! My, this is tasty grass! (*Hold puppet face toward floor; move mouth up and down.*) I see more yummy-looking grass under that bush. Munch! Munch! (*Hold puppet face toward floor; move mouth up and down.*) Time to move on. Oops! I'm caught. The bush won't let go of me. (*Move puppet frantically back and forth in struggling motions.*)

I'd better call my shepherd. B-a-a, b-a-a! (*Have puppet make sheep sounds.*) Where is my shepherd? Where are the other sheep? I was so busy eating this grass, I didn't see them leave. I have to get loose and catch up with them. (*Move puppet frantically back and forth.*) It's no use. I can't get loose from this bush, and nobody hears me. (*Make puppet hang head downward.*)

It's getting dark. I'm scared. What if a wolf or a bear finds me? What was that noise! (*Make puppet jump in fright.*)

It's my shepherd! He came back! Oh, thank goodness. Hey! I'm over here. B-a-a, b-a-a! (*Have puppet make sheep sounds.*)

Boy! I'm glad my shepherd found me. I learned a lesson. I'm going to stay with the flock, no matter how much tasty grass I see somewhere else.

Bible Matthew 18:10-14

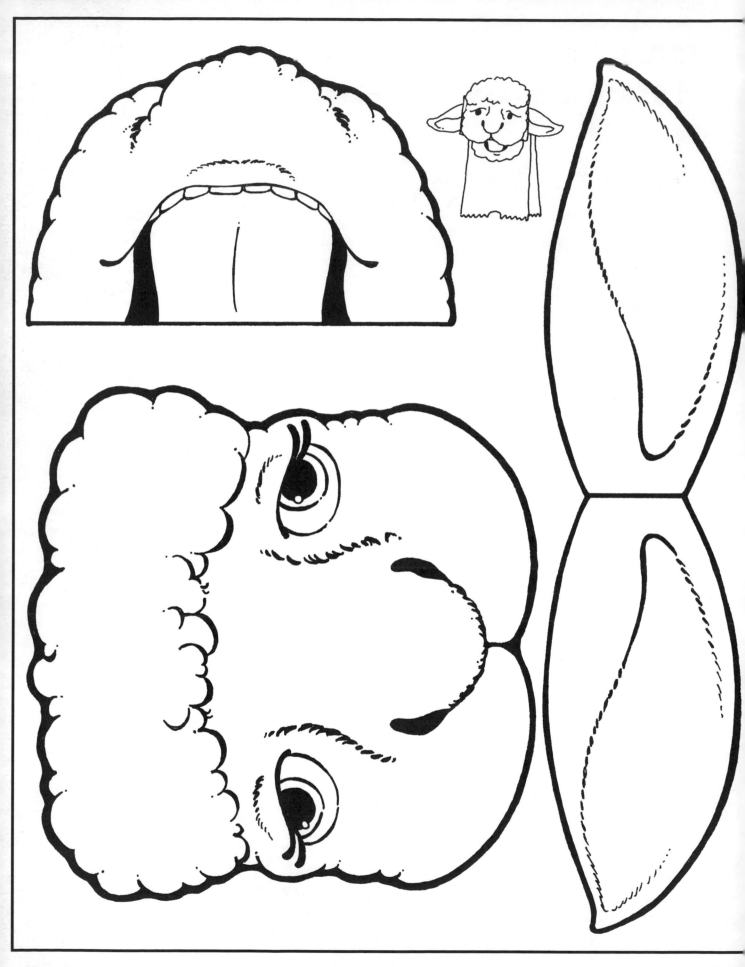

Easter

Craft 1

Supplies: Mary faces (see page 63), scissors, crayons, small paper plates, glue, craft sticks or tongue depressors, tape

Mary, Mary

Photocopy and cut out the two Mary faces (see page 63) for each child. Give each child both a sad face and a happy face. Let the children decorate the faces with crayons.

Give each child a small paper plate. Help the children glue the sad Mary face on one side of the paper plate and the happy Mary face on the opposite side of the paper plate. Or help the children glue the two faces back to back. Help each child make a handle for the puppet by gluing or taping a craft stick or tongue depressor to the plate or circle.

> **Say:** Jesus died and was buried in a tomb. Mary, a friend of Jesus, was sad that Jesus was dead. She went to the tomb, but Jesus was not in the tomb. Jesus was alive! Mary was surprised and happy. She ran to tell the other friends of Jesus that Jesus was alive!

Show the children how to hold the Mary puppets by the handle. Have the children turn the puppets to Mary's sad face.

> **Say:** When Mary went to the tomb, she was sad and unhappy.

Then turn the puppet to the happy face.

> **Say:** Mary was happy when she saw that Jesus was alive. Today we celebrate with joy because we know Jesus is alive.

Bible
Matthew
28:1-6

craft 2

Supplies: butterfly strips (see page 64), scissors, crayons or markers, glue or tape, green crepe paper

Butterflies Flutterby

Photocopy and cut apart the butterfly strips (see page 64) for each child. Give each child a strip.

Say: Butterflies can help us remember that God plans for new life. The butterfly begins life as a tiny egg. The egg hatches into a caterpillar. The caterpillar eats and eats and eats until the time is ready. Then it spins a cocoon and sleeps. While the caterpillar sleeps, its body changes into a new creature. It changes into a butterfly. When we see butterflies, we can remember new life and Jesus.

Let the children decorate the butterflies with crayons or markers. Show the children how to glue or tape the ends of each strip together to make a wrist band. Let the children glue or tape strips of green crepe paper to their wrist bands. Encourage the children to wear their wrist bands.

Read the litany printed below. Have the children wave their arms up and down like butterfly wings each time you say the refrain.

Say: Have you heard the good news?

Refrain:
Butterflies of every color,
Yellow, orange, and blue,
Remind us all that Jesus lives
And everything is new!

Jesus is not dead.
(*Say refrain.*)

Jesus is alive!
(*Say refrain.*)

See, everything has become new!
(*Say refrain.*)

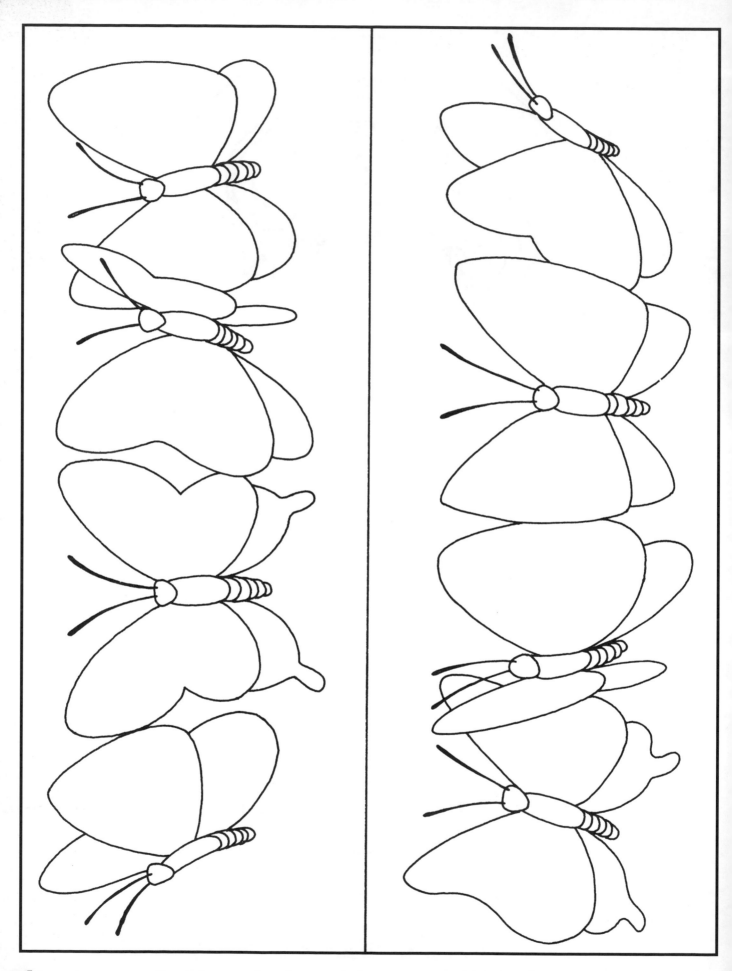

Two by Two

craft

Supplies: salt, water, cornstarch, saucepan, yarn, paper plates, paper towels, tempera paint, paintbrushes, permanent black marker

Follower Footprints

Before class, make a supply of hardening clay. Mix together 2 cups salt, 1 cup boiling water, and 1 cup cornstarch. Cook over low heat until mixture is stiff. Cool dough and knead until smooth. If you need to store the clay overnight, wrap it tightly in plastic wrap or seal it in an airtight container.

Tape a loop of yarn to the back of a paper plate for each child. Give each child a paper plate and enough clay to cover the bottom of it.

Say: Jesus sent his twelve special followers out to tell people about God's love and to ask them to follow Jesus. We can be like the special followers. Jesus' followers made footprints in the sand as they traveled from town to town. We can make footprints to remind us that we are followers of Jesus.

Encourage the children to spread out their clay until it covers the plate and to pat it flat. With a paper towel and water carefully clean off the bottoms of each child's shoes. Help each child gently step onto the clay with both feet to make footprints. Clean the child's shoes again with a paper towel and water.

Let the children paint the clay and footprints with tempera paint. With a permanent black marker write, "(*Child's name*) is a follower of Jesus." around the rim of each child's plate. The footprints will need to set overnight to dry. Set them aside to give to the children's parents or caregivers for safekeeping until they are dry.

Bible
Mark
6:6-7

The Last Supper

craft

Supplies: grape picture (see page 67); scissors; newspapers; paint smocks; paper towels; shallow tray; purple tempera paint; milk jug or juice jug lids, empty thread spools, film canisters, or cardboard rolls and tape; construction paper; purple and green crayons

Great Grapes

Photocopy and cut out the grape picture (see page 67). Give each child a copy. Let the children use green and purple crayons to decorate their grape pictures.

Say: Jesus shared a special meal with his friends. Jesus and his friends ate bread and drank juice from a cup at the special meal. The juice Jesus and his friends drank was made from grapes. Let's make pictures of grapes.

Give each child a piece of construction paper. Cover the work area with newspapers and have the children wear smocks to protect their clothing. Place paper towels into a shallow tray. Pour purple tempera paint onto the towels to make a paint pad.

Provide milk jug or juice jug lids, empty thread spools, film canisters, or cardboard rolls. If you use cardboard rolls, tape three cardboard rolls together. (These may be three toilet paper rolls or a paper towel roll cut into three pieces.)

Show the children how to press the ends of the items onto the paint pad and then onto their papers to make clusters of grapes. Let the children add a stem or leaves with a green crayon. Set the pictures aside to dry and have the children wash their hands.

Say: We drink grape juice at a special meal called Communion. When we drink the grape juice at Communion, we can remember that Jesus loves us.

Bible
Mark
14:22-26

Garden of Gethsemane

craft 1

Supplies: large piece of paper or construction paper and tape; glue; cupcake papers; tissue paper and scissors; crayons; green construction paper

Gardens Galore

Place a large piece of paper on the table or on the floor. Or tape the backs of several sheets of construction paper together.

Say: Today we're talking about Jesus and his friends. Jesus needed to talk to God. He asked his friends, Peter, James, and John, to go with him to a garden so that he could pray. Let's make a garden.

Let the children make a garden mural. Have the children make flowers for the mural in one of the following ways:

Cupcake papers: Let the children glue cupcake papers onto the mural paper.

Tissue paper: Cut colored tissue paper into squares. Show the children how to crumple the tissue paper. Let the children glue the crumpled papers onto the mural paper.

Handprints: Use crayons to trace each child's handprint onto the mural paper to represent flowers.

Cut green construction paper into one-inch strips. Show the children how to glue the strips onto the mural to make stems for the flowers. Let the children use crayons to add grass and sky. Mount the garden mural on a wall.

Bible
Mark
14:32-42

craft 2

Supplies: praying hands (see page 70); scissors; crayons, glitter glue, or glitter crayons; paper plates; glue; paper punch; yarn

A Plateful of Prayers

Photocopy the praying hands (see page 70) for each child. Cut out the praying hands around the circle and the prayer poem printed with the praying hands.

Give each child a praying hands circle. Let the children decorate the praying hands with crayons, glitter glue, or glitter crayons.

Give each child a paper plate. You may want to use inexpensive white paper plates, or purchase gold or silver paper plates. These paper plates may be found at party stores in the wedding anniversary section. Let the children glue their praying hands circles inside the paper plates.

Give each child a prayer poem. Let the children glue the prayer poems on the backs of their paper plates. Use a paper punch to punch a hole in the top of each paper plate. Tie a loop of yarn through each plate to make a hanger.

> **Say:** Jesus needed to talk to God. He asked his friends, Peter, James, and John, to go with him to a garden so that he could pray. Prayer is a way we can talk to God. Jesus knew that he could pray to God and that God would hear his prayer and help him know what to do.

Say the prayer poem for the children.

© 1998 Abingdon Press.

69

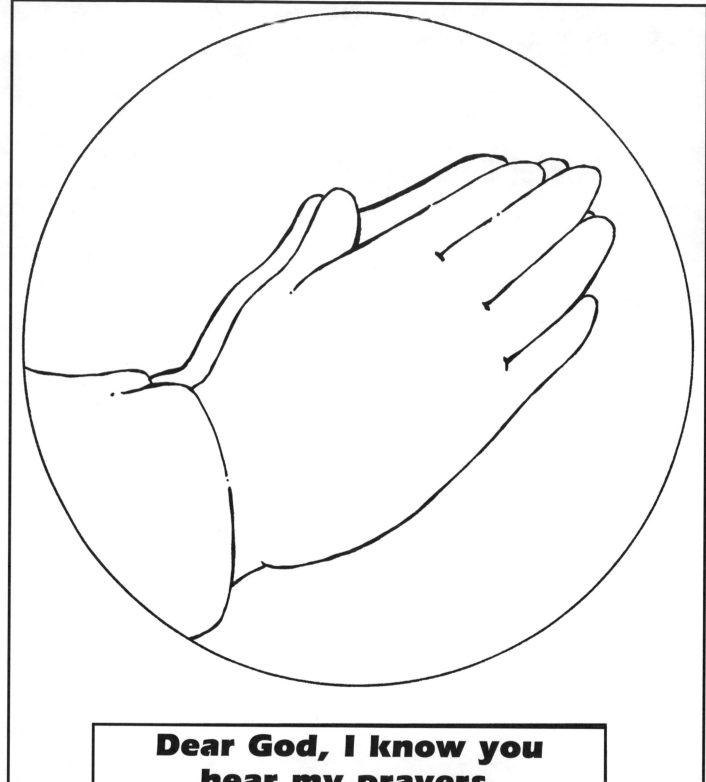

Dear God, I know you hear my prayers. I know you love me too. Help me be kind and loving in everything I do.

A Baby Is Coming

craft

Supplies: angel pattern (see page 72); scissors; lunch-size paper bags; paper doilies, Christmas wrapping paper, or construction paper; crayons or markers; glue

Heavenly Wraps

Photocopy the angel pattern (see page 72). Use the pattern to cut lunch-size paper bags into angel shapes, one for each child. Cut wings out of paper doilies, Christmas wrapping paper, or construction paper. Show the children the angel bags.

Say: Today we're talking about Mary and an angel. The angel had a special message for Mary. The angel told Mary the good news that she would have a baby named Jesus.

Give each child a paper bag. Let the children use crayons or markers to decorate both sides of the angel bags.

Give each child the wings cut from doilies, Christmas wrapping paper, or construction paper. Help the children glue the wings onto the backs of the angel bags. Write the children's names on the bags. Show the children how the bags will open to make the angels stand.

Bible
Luke
1:26–31

Jesus' Birth

craft 1

Supplies: foil cupcake liners or plastic lids from potato chip, yogurt, or margarine containers; aluminum foil; colored tissue paper; glue; glue brush; paper punch, yarn

Foil Frolics

Say: When Mary and Joseph got to Bethlehem, baby Jesus was born. We celebrate baby Jesus' birthday on Christmas. People all over the world celebrate Jesus' birthday. One of the ways people in Mexico celebrate Jesus' birthday is by making Christmas ornaments.

Give each child a foil cupcake liner. Have the children flatten the liners. Or wrap a plastic lid from potato chip, yogurt, or margarine containers with aluminum foil for each child.

Let the children decorate the foil liners or lids with colored tissue paper. Tear tissue paper into small pieces. Have the children brush glue over the liners or lids and then place the tissue paper on the glue. Let the ornaments dry.

Use a paper punch to make a hole in the top of each ornament. Tie a loop of yarn through the hole to make a hanger.

Bible
Luke
2:1-7

craft 2

Supplies: parrot face, wings, and tail (see page 75); scissors; crayons or markers; paper bags; colored tissue paper, crepe paper, or construction paper; glue; small boxes of raisins, sugarless gum, or other treats; newspaper; yarn or string; broom handle or large dowel; plastic bat; large bowl or paper bag; small resealable plastic bags

Pinata Party

Photocopy and cut out the parrot face, wings, and tail (see page 75). Let the children decorate the cutouts with crayons or markers.

Say: We celebrate baby Jesus' birthday on Christmas. People in a country called Mexico play a game with piñatas. A piñata is filled with treats for the children. When the piñata is broken, the treats fall down for the children to enjoy.

Let the children help you glue the parrot face, wings, and tail onto a paper bag. Have the children tear colored tissue paper, crepe paper, or construction paper into small pieces. Let the children glue the pieces all over the bag. Poke holes in the paper bag to make it easier to break. Place small boxes of raisins, sugarless gum, and other treats into the bag. Crumple newspaper and place it inside the bag to help fill the bag. Tie the bag closed with yarn or string.

Hang the piñata from the ceiling or tie the piñata to a broom handle or large dowel. If you choose to hang it from a handle or dowel, have another adult available to hold the handle or dowel.

Have the children sit in a wide circle on the floor around the piñata. Make it clear to the children that they must stay seated until the piñata is broken.

Plan for either you or another adult to break the piñata. Stand in the center of the circle with a plastic bat. Turn around several times. Encourage the children to give you directions for how to hit the piñata with the bat.

Ask: Should I step backwards? Should I swing higher? Should I step forward? Should I swing lower?

Keep your eyes open as you swing. Be aware of the children around you. If the children start to move, stop and remind them to stay seated until the piñata is broken.

When the piñata breaks, let the children move to pick up the treats. Have the children place all the treats in a large bowl or paper bag. Have the children sit around a table or in a circle on the floor. Give each child a self-sealing plastic bag. Divide the treats among the children and help them put the treats in their bags to take home.

The Shepherds' Visit

craft

Supplies: shepherd picture (see page 77), crayons or markers, scissors, dark blue or black construction paper, glue, shallow tray or box lid, glitter (optional: angel-shaped glitter)

A Sky Full of Angels

Photocopy the shepherd picture (see page 77) for each child.

Say: Today we're talking about shepherds who were watching their sheep the night baby Jesus was born. A shepherd takes care of sheep. Find the sheep in your pictures. Find the shepherds in your pictures.

Let the children decorate their pictures with crayons or markers. Encourage them to color the sky to be a nighttime sky. Or cut around each shepherd picture. Give each child a piece of dark blue or black construction paper. Let the children glue their shepherd pictures onto the construction paper.

Say: While the shepherds were watching their sheep, an angel appeared in the sky. The angel told the shepherds the good news that baby Jesus was born. Suddenly the sky was filled with angels singing their praise to God. Let's add angels to our shepherd pictures.

Show the children how to spread glue all over the sky part of their pictures. Place each picture in a shallow tray or box lid.

Show the child how to sprinkle the glitter over the glue. Shake the picture over the tray or box lid. Save any extra glitter to use with the next child. Let the pictures dry flat.

Say: The shepherds hurried to see baby Jesus. They praised God for baby Jesus and told others the good news.

Bible
Luke
2:8–20

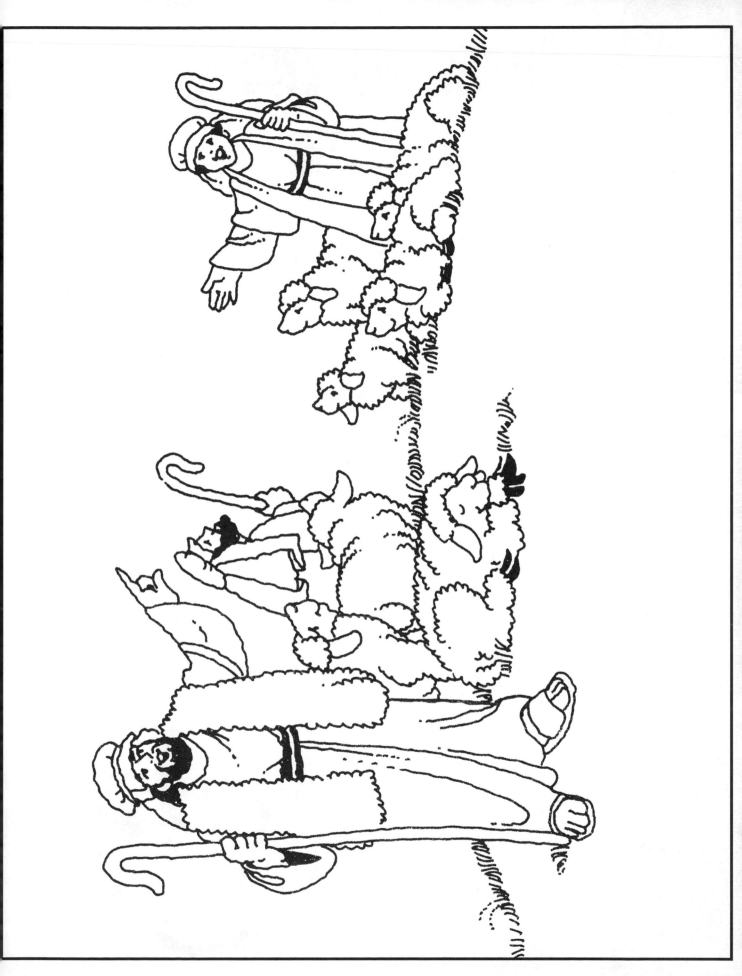

Jesus in the Synagogue

craft

Supplies: good news scroll (see page 79), crayons or markers, scissors, paper grocery bags

Good News Scrolls

Photocopy the good news scroll (see page 79) for each child. Let the children decorate the scrolls with crayons or markers.

Say: Jesus grew from a baby to a boy to a man. When Jesus was a man, he went to the synagogue in his hometown. A synagogue is a place where Bible-times people went to worship and to learn about God. The synagogue was an important building, just as our church building is an important building.

Cut paper grocery bags into 9-by-12-inch rectangles. Give each child a paper bag rectangle. Show the children how to scrunch the paper bag into a ball. Then show the children how to smooth the paper bag flat again.

Repeat this process several times. This will make the paper bag feel like leather or parchment paper. Have the children glue their good news scrolls onto the wrinkled paper bag rectangles.

If you do not have paper bags, the children may wrinkle their good news scroll paper. Have the children smooth the scroll paper flat. Let the children color the plain side of the wrinkled paper with crayons to make their scrolls look like parchment.

Bible
Luke
4:16-22

God

You!

News!

Good

Loves

Bible—Times Fishermen

craft 1

Supplies: fish page (see page 82), large shoebox, light blue construction paper, posterboard or card stock, glue, glitter, lunch-size paper bags, string, craft sticks, tape (optional: sequins)

Classroom Aquarium

Although this activity calls for extra before-class preparation, the children's enjoyment of the completed project can make it worth your efforts.

Before class line a large shoebox with light blue construction paper. Make a copy of the page of fish (see page 82) and glue it to posterboard or card stock (an old file folder works well).

Cut out as many of the fish as you have class members. Pour a different color of glitter into each of three or four lunch-size paper bags. Cut string or ⅛-inch strips of the blue construction paper into varying lengths from one inch to five inches. Have one ready for each fish.

Give each child a fish and let the children decorate their fish with glitter. A good way to do so with young children is to give each one a craft stick. Then put a good-sized spot of glue on each fish and invite the child to spread it around with the craft stick.

When the children have glue where they want it, let them choose which color glitter they want on their fish. Put each fish in the bag with the chosen color of glitter, show the child how to hold the bag tightly closed at the top, and let the child shake the bag. Pull out the glittered fish.

As an option, have sequins on hand and invite each child to choose a sequin for you to glue on the fish for an eye.

Bible
Luke
5:1-11

Tape one end of a piece of string or a strip of construction paper to the back of each fish. Tape the other end to the inside of one side of the box. (If you are using construction paper instead of string, fold the end opposite the fish into a right angle and tape the short side of the angle to the box.)

Be sure to spread the fish out evenly as you tape, taping some toward the back of the box, some in the middle, and some toward the front.

Lay the box on the side opposite the side to which you taped fish and see the layers of fish "swimming" in the aquarium.

Say: The Bible tells us stories about Jesus calling people to follow him. First he called four fishermen friends to follow.

craft 2

Supplies: scissors, plastic sandwich bags, tissue paper in different colors, clear tape

Fish—Tish

Before class use sharp scissors to slit along the edges of the folded-back part of each sandwich bag and unfold it. Give each child a bag to make a see-through fish.

Stack the tissue paper in colors on the table. Invite the children to tear the tissue paper into pieces bigger than their hands. Show the children how to loosely crumple these pieces. Let each child fill her or his bag with crumpled tissue. Gather the open end of each bag and wrap clear tape around the gathers about two inches from the open edge. Fan out the resulting "tail."

Say: Men who were catching fish decided to be followers of Jesus.

Birds of the Air

craft

Supplies: birds and flowers pictures (see page 84), crayons or markers, glue or tape

Birds and Flowers

Photocopy the birds and flowers pictures (see page 84) for each child. Let the children decorate the pictures with crayons or markers.

Help each child fold the page along the dotted line. Glue or tape the sides of each page together, leaving the bottom open. Show each child how to place a hand inside the bottom to make a turnaround puppet.

Say: Jesus told about how God loves and cares for us. Jesus told his friends that God cares about the birds and flowers. Then Jesus told his friends that God cares even more about people.

Sing the song below to the tune of "Twinkle, Twinkle, Little Star." Have the children hold up the bird sides of their puppets when you sing the verse about birds. Have the children turn their puppets to their flower sides when you sing about flowers.

Birdies, birdies, everywhere,
Tell us of God's love and care.
See them high up in the sky,
Ducks and redbirds flying by.
Birdies, birdies, everywhere,
Tell us of God's love and care.

Flowers, flowers, everywhere,
Tell us of God's love and care.
Growing in their flower beds,
Blue and yellow, orange and red.
Flowers, flowers, everywhere,
Tell us of God's love and care.

Bible
Luke
12:22-26

Zacchaeus

craft

Supplies: leaves, paper, glue, clear self-adhesive paper

Make a Leaf Table Mat

Say: Today we're hearing about Zacchaeus, who climbed a tree in order to see Jesus.

If it is possible, take the children on a walk to look at trees. If you have sycamore trees in your area, point out the tree to the children.

Collect leaves as you walk, or if you decide not to take the walk, collect leaves before class begins. Let the children make a leaf collage from the collection.

Give each child a piece of paper. Let the children glue the leaves onto the paper. Cover the paper with clear self-adhesive paper.

Remind the children that Jesus loved Zacchaeus and changed Zacchaeus's life.

Say: Jesus loves you too. Jesus loves everyone!

Bible
Luke
19:1–8

Jesus' Baptism

Craft 1

Supplies: heavy-duty, self-sealing plastic bags; blue hair gel; tape

Water Works

Fill heavy-duty, self-sealing plastic bags full of blue hair gel. Seal the bags and then tape them closed. Chill the bags in a refrigerator. Let each child hold his or her bag and squeeze it. Tell the children that the bags remind you of water. Talk about the different ways you use water (to drink, to take a bath, to water the plants, and so forth). Tell the children that Jesus was baptized with water in the river.

© 1997 Abingdon Press.

Craft 2

Supplies: dove picture (see page 87), newspaper, paint smocks, paper towels, shallow container, white tempera paint, hand-washing supplies

Fine Feathers

Photocopy the dove picture (see page 87) for each child. Give each child a picture. Cover the table with newspaper and have the children wear paint smocks. Fold paper towels and place them in the bottom of a shallow container. Pour white tempera paint onto the paper towels to make a paint pad.

Show the children how to press their thumbs onto the paint pad and then onto their doves to make thumbprints. The prints will make the feathers for the doves. Set the pictures flat to dry. Have the children wash their hands.

Say: Jesus grew from a baby to a boy to a man. When Jesus was a man, he was baptized with water from a river. As Jesus was baptized, a dove flew down from the sky. Jesus knew that God loved him and that he was God's son.

Bible
John
1:29–34

86

87

A Wedding at Cana

Craft 1

Supplies: green construction paper; scissors; tape; green paper, real leaves or silk leaves; glue; masking tape

Groom Garlands

Cut green construction paper into two-by-twelve-inch bands. Tape two bands together to make one long band. Give each child one long band.

Say: In Bible times, men who were going to get married wore a kind of headband called a garland on their heads at their weddings. The Bible tells a story about a wedding that Jesus went to. Maybe the groom was wearing a garland. Garland headbands were made of leaves. We can make garlands to wear.

Let the children add leaves to the bands in one of the following ways:

Leaf shapes: Draw simple leaf shapes on green paper or trace around a real leaf several times. Help the children cut out the leaves and glue them to their bands.

Real leaves: Gather real tree leaves and help the children tape or glue them to the green bands.

Silk leaves: Purchase silk leaves from a craft store or floral supply outlet. Let the children glue the leaves to their bands.

Size each child's garland to her or his head and tape the ends together. Put a strip of masking tape around the inside of each garland to help keep it from tearing.

Bible
John
2:1-11

Craft 2

Supplies: Bible verse page (see page 90), scissors, colored tissue paper, plastic sheeting, bowls of water, paintbrushes, clear self-adhesive paper (optional: hair dryer)

Party Praise Mats

Cut colored tissue paper into three- or four-inch squares. Cover the table with plastic. Put the tissue paper, bowls of water, and paintbrushes in the center of the table. Give each child a copy of the page with the Bible verse surrounded by water jars (see page 90).

> **Say:** Our Bible verse is "Let the peoples praise you, O God; let all the peoples praise you" (Psalm 67:3). We can make place mats to remind us of the Bible verse every time we use them. Our place mats will have jars on them like the jars that held water in Bible times.

Show each child how to lay a piece of tissue paper on his or her paper, paint over it with water, and lift it off to see the color that has bled through to the paper. Encourage the children to use several colors of tissue on their place mats to make them colorful. Point out how the colors change when the colors overlap.

Be sure that the children's names are on their place mats. Set the place mats aside to dry. If you have a helper, using a hair dryer shortens the drying time. Pour out the water and collect all the soggy tissue into one bowl.

When the place mats have dried, cut two pieces of clear self-adhesive paper about one-fourth inch longer and wider than the paper. Laminate each place mat between two sheets of self-adhesive paper by laying one piece of self-adhesive paper sticky-side up on the table and pressing the mat onto it. Turn the mat over and press it onto the second sheet of self-adhesive paper placed sticky-side up on the table.

> **Say:** In Bible times people had parties to celebrate weddings and to praise God for the new family that was getting started.

Let the peoples
praise you, O God;
let all the peoples
praise you.

Psalm 67:3

Man Beside the Pool

craft

Supplies: man beside the pool (see page 92), crayons, grocery-size paper bags, scissors, construction paper or rolled paper, glue

Mat Man

Photocopy the picture of the man beside the pool (see page 92) for each child. Give each child a picture. Let the children decorate the pictures with crayons.

Say: Today we're hearing about Jesus and a man who could not walk. He lay on a mat beside a pool, hoping someone would help him get into the swirling waters of the pool. (*Point to the man and the pool.*) He thought the swirling waters would heal him. Jesus helped the man. (*Point to Jesus.*) Jesus did not help the man by putting him into the swirling waters. Jesus helped the man by healing him. Jesus told the man to take up his mat and walk! The man could walk! The man was glad that Jesus helped him. We can help people today. One important way we can help others is by praying for them.

Say: Let's make our own Bible-times mat.

Cut the side from a paper bag for each child. Or use a large piece of construction paper or rolled paper. Give each child the paper.

Show the children how to crumple the paper into a ball and smooth the paper back out again. This will soften the paper to make it feel like cloth. Have the children glue their pictures onto the paper.

© 1998 Abingdon Press.

Bible
John
5:2-9

92

The Foot Washing

craft

Supplies: picture of Jesus washing his friends' feet (see page 94); wet sponge; colored chalk, crayons, or markers

Clean Cool Color

Photocopy the picture of Jesus washing his friend's feet (see page 94) for each child. Give each child a picture.

Say: In Bible times people wore sandals without socks or went barefoot. When they walked on the dirt roads, their feet got dusty and dirty. Whenever they went inside a house to eat, they left their dusty sandals at the door. They wanted their feet to be clean and cool before they ate. Sometimes there were servants to wash their feet, and sometimes friends took turns washing each other's feet.

Wipe over each child's paper with a wet sponge. Let the children draw over the wet paper with colored chalk. Set the picture aside to dry completely. Or let the children decorate the pictures with crayons or markers.

Say: Today we're talking about the time when Jesus washed his friends' feet to show his love for his friends. He wanted his friends to remember him and to remember how much he loved them.

Permission granted to photocopy for local church use. © 1999 Abingdon Press.

The Great Commission

Craft

Supplies: mural paper, felt-tip marker, construction paper, glue, crayons or markers, safety scissors

Footprints on the Wall

Cut a piece of mural paper three feet wide and write the Bible verse, "You will tell everyone about me everywhere in the world" (Acts 1:8, *Good News Bible*, paraphrased), in the center of it with a felt-tip marker.

Have the children trace around their feet on pieces of construction paper. Let the children cut out their footprints and glue them onto the mural.

If you have very young children, you will need to cut the footprints out for them. Or trace their footprints directly onto the mural paper and let the children color their footprints with crayons or markers. Display the mural on a wall.

Say: The followers of Jesus went many places to help others and to tell others about Jesus.

Paul

craft 1

Supplies: "Paul's Little Instruction Book" (see page 98), scissors, crayons or markers

Paul's Little Instruction Book

Copy the "Paul's Little Instruction Book" pages (see page 98) for each child. Fold the page along the solid lines like a greeting card for each child.

Give each child the cover of the book. Let the children decorate the covers with crayons or markers.

Say: Today we're hearing about a man named Paul. Paul did not like the followers of Jesus. But when Paul saw the bright light and heard the voice of Jesus, he made a change. He became a follower of Jesus.

Have the children open their books to the inside pages. Let the children decorate these pages with crayons or markers.

Say: When Paul became a follower of Jesus, he learned what Jesus wanted him to do. We can find some of the things that Paul learned in our Bible. Paul learned that love is kind. He learned that love never ends.

Have the children repeat the Bible verses. Have the children turn their books to the last page. Write the children's names in the spaces provided. Let the children decorate the page with crayons or markers.

Say: Paul became a follower of Jesus. We can be followers of Jesus, just like Paul.

© 1997 Abingdon Press.

Bible
Acts
9:1–9

craft z

Supplies: newspaper, paint smocks, construction paper, crayons, yellow tempera paint, plastic containers, water, paintbrushes

Bright Lights

Cover the work area with newspapers and have the children wear smocks to protect their clothing.

Give each child a piece of construction paper. Have the children color the papers with crayons. Encourage the children to bear down on the crayons to make heavy lines.

Pour yellow tempera paint into plastic containers. Thin the paint with water. Show the children how to brush the paint over their crayon pictures.

Encourage the children to cover their entire pictures with the paint.

Use this activity when you tell the children about Paul. Remind the children that Paul saw a bright light and heard Jesus talking to him. Paul became a follower of Jesus.

   Say: The yellow paint reminds us of the bright light.

Love
never
ends.

1 Corinthians 13:8

Love
is
kind,

1 Corinthians 13:4

Name

Paul's Little
Instruction Book

Dorcas

craft 1

Supplies: robe (see page 100), yarn, scissors, glue, shallow pans

Robe—a—Rama

Photocopy the robe (see page 100) for each child. Let the children decorate the robes with yarn. Cut yarn into six-inch lengths. Pour glue into shallow pans. Show the children how to drag yarn through the glue and then place the yarn on their paper robes. Set the robes aside to dry.

Say: Dorcas was a follower of Jesus. She sewed robes and clothing for people in need. Dorcas knew that followers of Jesus shared with others.

© 1997 Abingdon Press.

craft 2

Supplies: simple clothing shapes cut from old file folders or other light cardboard, paper punch, yarn, clear tape

Sewing Cards

Remind your children that Dorcas, a follower of Jesus, made clothes for other people who needed them. Cut simple shapes of clothing (coats, pants, dresses) from old file folders or other light cardboard.

Punch ten or twelve holes around the edges of each clothing shape.

Give your children lengths of yarn with clear tape wrapped around one end. Show the children how to poke the yarn in and out of the holes to "sew" the garment.

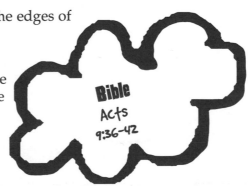

Bible
Acts
9:36-42

© 2000 Abingdon Press.

Permission granted to photocopy for local church use. © 1997 Abingdon Press.

Timothy, Eunice, and Lois

craft

Supplies: pictures of people cut from clothing catalogs and department store flyers, construction paper, marker, glue sticks

Family Pictures

Before class cut out a variety of pictures of men, women, boys, and girls from clothing catalogs, department store flyers, and so forth. Include pictures of babies and people who are old enough to be grandparents.

Write "My Family" at the top of a sheet of construction paper for each child.

Place glue sticks and all of the pictures you have cut out on the work table. Give each child a sheet of construction paper with "My Family" written at the top.

Say: Today we're talking about a boy named Timothy and his mother and his grandmother. Timothy learned about God and Jesus in his family. You have a family, just as Timothy did.

Invite the children to find pictures of the people in their families and to glue the pictures on their construction paper. Help the children write the names of the family members under the selected pictures.

© 2000 Abingdon Press.

Bible
Acts 16:1–3;
1 Timothy 1:5

101

Lydia

Craft 1

Supplies: flour, glue, cornstarch, water, red and blue food coloring, airtight container

Purple Goop

Make purple goop. Mix together 1 cup flour, 1 cup cornstarch, and ½ cup glue. Add red and blue food coloring to water to make purple. Add the water mixture as needed to make the dough pliable.

Remind your children that Lydia sold purple cloth.

Store the purple goop in an airtight container.

Craft 2

Supplies: flour, water, Kool-Aid drink mix (purple), corn oil, salt, alum

Purple Play Dough

Make purple play dough. Mix together 2½ to 3 cups flour, one package purple Kool-Aid drink mix, 2 cups boiling water, 3 tablespoons corn oil, ½ cup water, and 1 tablespoon alum. Knead with flour. (It may take up to one cup more flour.) This play dough has a nice fragrance, is very colorful, and is soft and flexible.

Remind your children that Lydia sold purple cloth.

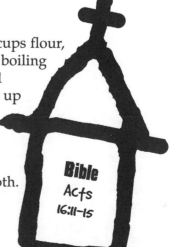

Bible
Acts
16:11–15

Priscilla and Aquila

Craft 1

Supplies: Paul, Priscilla, and Aquila picture (see page 104); scissors; crayons or markers; paper plates; glue; paper punch; yarn; clear tape

Sew Happy

Photocopy the Paul, Priscilla, and Aquila picture (see page 104) for each child. Cut each picture out along the circle. Let the children decorate the pictures with crayons or markers.

> **Say:** Today we're talking about three followers of Jesus named Paul, Priscilla, and Aquila. Paul traveled to many cities. Sometimes he stayed with Priscilla and Aquila. Paul, Priscilla, and Aquila worked together making tents. The three friends also worked together telling others about Jesus.

Give each child a paper plate. Show the children how to glue their picture circles in the center of the paper plates. Use a paper punch to punch holes around the edges of the plates. Make the holes far enough away from the edges so that they will not tear.

Give each child a length of yarn about twelve inches long. Wrap one end of the yarn with tape. Show the children how to lace the length of yarn through the holes around the paper plates. When the children have finished lacing, tie off the ends of their yarn.

© 1999 Abingdon Press.

Craft 2

Supplies: plastic-foam meat trays, pencil or paper punch, yarn, plastic needle

A Stitch in Time

Punch holes in the trays with a pencil or paper punch. Thread yarn through the plastic needle. Let the children push the needle and yarn in and out of the holes. Remind the children that Paul, Priscilla, and Aquila worked together to make tents. The three friends also worked together to tell others about Jesus.

Bible
Acts
18:1-3

© 1999 Abingdon Press.

Paul's Shipwreck

craft

Supplies: Bible verse page (see page 106), crayons, construction paper, stapler and staples, tissues or old newspapers

Pillow Talk

Photocopy the Bible verse page (see page 106) for each child. Let the children decorate the pages with crayons. Read the Bible verse to the children.

Say: Today we're talking about Paul. Paul was traveling by boat when a big storm came over the water. The boat fell apart, but everyone swam safely to shore. Even during the storm Paul told others about Jesus. Paul knew that love never gives up. He never gave up telling others about Jesus.

Let the children make pillows. Give each child a piece of construction paper. Place the Bible verse page on top of the construction paper. Help each child staple three edges of the papers together, leaving a fourth edge open.

Show the children how to crumple tissues or old newspapers and then stuff the papers into their pillows. Staple the opening together.

Say: Our pillows can help us remember that love never gives up.

Bible
Acts
27:13-44

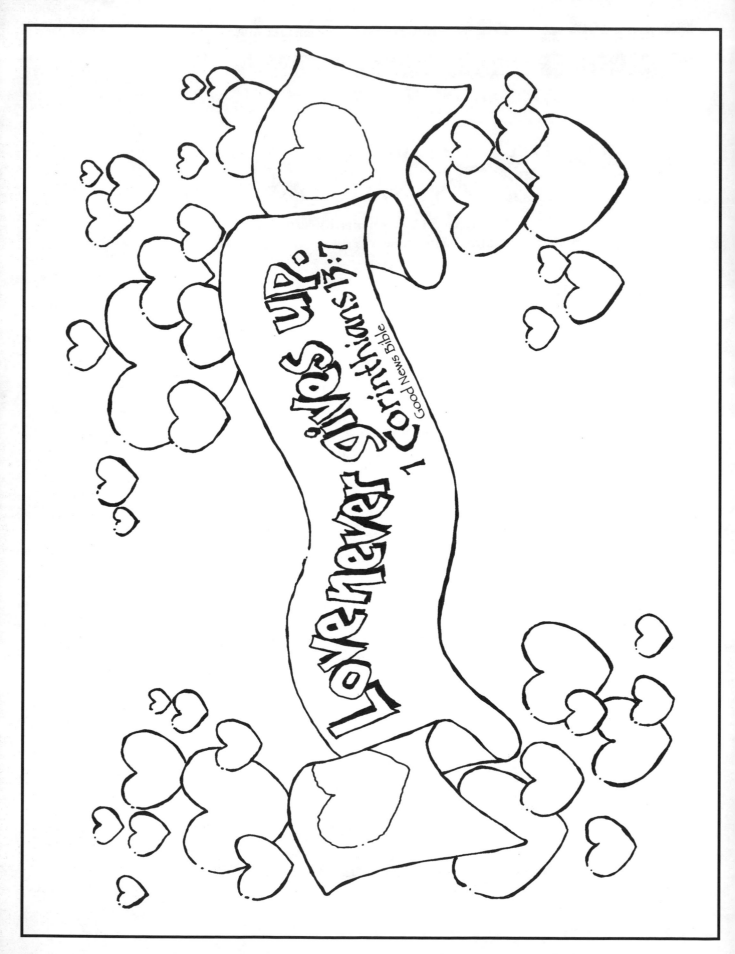

Love never gives up.
1 Corinthians 13:7
Good News Bible

Fruits of the Spirit

Craft 1

Supplies: fruit pictures (see page 109), safety scissors, paper punch, crayons or markers, yarn, drinking straws

Great Garlands

Photocopy and cut apart several copies of the fruit pictures (see page 109). Use a paper punch to punch a hole in the top of each picture. Let the children decorate the pictures with crayons or markers.

Cut yarn into 18-inch lengths. Give the children several drinking straws. Show the children how to cut the drinking straws into smaller pieces using safety scissors. Then show the children how to string the straws and the fruit pictures onto the yarn. If you wrap one end of the yarn with tape, it will be easier to string the straw pieces and fruit pictures together.

When the children have finished, tie each length of yarn together to make a garland. Hang the garland in your room.

   Say: The fruit pictures can help us remember that love is a fruit of the Spirit.

Craft 2

Supplies: earth picture (see page 110), crayons, thinned blue tempera paint, plastic containers, paintbrushes, newspapers, smocks

All the Earth

Photocopy the earth picture (see page 110) for each child. Cover the tables with newspaper and have the children wear smocks to protect their clothing. Let the children decorate their

Bible
Galatians
5:22–23;
Psalm 98:4

pictures with crayons. Encourage the children to make heavy marks with the crayons.

Thin blue tempera paint with water. Pour the thinned paint into plastic containers. Let the children brush the paint all over their pictures. The crayons markings will show through the paint wash.

Read the Bible verse to the children.

Say: Joy is a fruit of the Spirit.

© 1999 Abingdon Press.

craft 3

Supplies: paper; crayons or markers; glue or tape; yarn or chenille stems; real flowers, damp paper towels and aluminum foil; or artificial or paper flowers; paper punch

Kindness Cones

Give each child a piece of paper. Let the children decorate their paper with crayons or markers. Help the children roll the paper into a cone shape and glue or tape the edges in place. Make a handle with yarn or a chenille stem. Make a hole on each side of the cone. Thread the yarn or chenille stem through the holes. The cone will now look like a basket with a handle.

Wrap the stems of real flowers in damp paper towels. Then cover the paper towels with aluminum foil. Place the flowers in the cone. Or let the children place artificial or paper flowers in the cone.

Take the children to an adult classroom. Let the children present the cones of flowers as a surprise.

© 1999 Abingdon Press.

Sing for joy to the Lord!
all the earth.
Psalm 98:4 Good News Bible

Index by Bible Reference

Index by Subject